# Talk Up Your Business

# Talk Up Your Business

How to make the most of opportunities to
promote and grow your small business

Mary Morel

First published in 2005

Copyright © Mary Morel 2005

All rights reserved. No part of this book may be reproduced or transmitted in any form or by any means, electronic or mechanical, including photocopying, recording or by any information storage and retrieval system, without prior permission in writing from the publisher. The *Australian Copyright Act 1968* (the Act) allows a maximum of one chapter or 10 per cent of this book, whichever is the greater, to be photocopied by any educational institution for its educational purposes provided that the educational institution (or body that administers it) has given a remuneration notice to Copyright Agency Limited (CAL) under the Act.

Allen & Unwin
83 Alexander Street
Crows Nest NSW 2065
Australia
Phone: (61 2) 8425 0100
Fax:    (61 2) 9906 2218
Email: info@allenandunwin.com
Web:   www.allenandunwin.com

National Library of Australia
Cataloguing-in-Publication entry:

Morel, Mary, 1950- .
Talk up your business : how to make the most of opportunities to promote and grow your small business.

Bibliography.
Includes index.
ISBN 1 74114 423 X.

1. Small business - Public relations. 2. Marketing. 3. Sales promotion. I. Title.

659.281

Set in 11/15 pt Stempel Garamond by Bookhouse, Sydney
Printed in Australia by Southwood Press, Sydney

10 9 8 7 6 5 4 3 2 1

# Contents

Preface   vii
Introduction   ix

1. Planning   1
2. What do you do?   15
3. Word of mouth and referrals   31
4. Networking   53
5. Telemarketing   77
6. Public speaking   104
7. Running seminars   127
8. More ways to talk up your business   150
9. Grow your business from within   161

References   179
Index   184

# Preface

My aim in writing this book and my previous book *Promote Your Business: How to write effective marketing material for your small business* is to provide practical, workable advice to small businesses wishing to promote and grow their businesses. Both books are based on personal experience, running seminars, talking to other small business owners and reading widely.

The process of learning about business planning, marketing and systems has transformed my business. When I first started my business, I was a freelance writer and took whatever work came my way. I was lucky that I knew a lot of people (I didn't in those days think in terms of 'networking') and received some interesting work. After a while, I became bored with some of the work, but didn't know how to change direction, so continued to accept everything that came my way and prided myself on my 'can do' attitude.

Moving countries was an opportunity to change the direction of my business, but as I no longer had a network and knew nothing about marketing, I sat in my lonely office fretting over my lack of work. It was time to go back to basics and learn about business planning, budgeting, business systems and marketing. Through learning and applying these skills, new opportunities have opened up for me and my business has grown in the direction I want to go.

I've learnt about the importance of having a clear strategy before I start doing any marketing. For me, that has meant being clear about what I offer, identifying my target markets, and using marketing tools I enjoy. I've discovered what marketing works best for me by experimenting and measuring my results. I've also found that if I take a more detached approach towards marketing and think about developing a relationship with a prospect rather than making a sales pitch, I enjoy the sales process more and get better results.

I now have a much better understanding of the benefits of business systems. The 'back end' of my business is in better shape and I outsource some tasks rather than doing everything myself.

My business continues to evolve, which is one of the reasons I love being self-employed. There's more information about my business, The M Factor, at http://www.themfactor.com. On my site, you can read several of my articles and sign up for my free e-newsletter *Factorial* on writing and marketing.

# Introduction

Growing your business in the direction you want to go, and at a speed you're comfortable with, requires planning. Each year, or more often if you're making major changes, you need to re-set your goals, re-evaluate your business and marketing plans, and work out a budget.

Part of this planning process involves working out what products and services you will continue offering, what you want to ditch and what new ones you plan to develop. Often, new ideas take time to jell, so be patient with yourself if you don't have instant clarity. Proceed with the new products or services you are sure of and allow the seedling thoughts to either develop further or wither.

Write down your plans so you crystallise your thoughts and also so you can communicate your ideas more easily to others involved in your business—your staff, coach or mentor. Writing down your ideas and sharing them with others also helps them become a reality. The more you imagine something, the more possible it seems.

Planning is fun. Next comes the hard—though ultimately the most satisfying—part, which is putting your plan into action so your goals become a reality. You need to deliver high-quality products and services and have efficient processes and systems in place so your business runs smoothly and doesn't take over your whole life.

Marketing is essential to grow your business. Even established businesses need to continually market themselves to maintain and grow their position in the marketplace. The main emphasis in this book, as in my earlier book *Promote Your Business*, is on marketing. But this book also looks at goal-setting and how to continue to develop your own skills and business systems so you are in control of your business and enjoy the journey.

## Business case studies

Throughout this book, I use three fictitious businesses to illustrate various approaches to marketing that retail, hospitality and service businesses could use to promote their businesses. The three businesses are: Delite Landscape Design, Blue Gum Restaurant, and Jane Amos, natural therapist. The first two of these case studies were also used in *Promote Your Business*.

### Delite Landscape Design

Delite Landscape Design has branches in three cities. Each branch combines boutique gardening stores with domestic and commercial landscape design and gardening services. The stores carry popular ranges of plants, such as camellias and roses, and some gardening accessories, such as hoses and fertilisers.

Delite Landscape Design also provides domestic and commercial landscape design services. The design work ranges from small backyards to large new property developments. Delite provides gardening and maintenance services for both commercial and residential properties.

The business was founded 27 years ago by qualified landscape designer John Pettit, and each branch employs at least one full-time landscape designer and retail and gardening staff. Some gardening staff are full time while others are employed on a casual basis over spring and summer.

## Blue Gum Restaurant

Blue Gum Restaurant is located close to the heart of the city and caters for both families and the business community. It serves modern cuisine at mid-range prices and is fully licensed as well as offering BYO. The restaurant has a function room which is used for corporate functions, and it now also offers a dial-a-dinner service.

Blue Gum Restaurant was established 12 years ago by a husband and wife team, Tania James and Bill Johnson. Tania works in the restaurant full time, managing the dining room and staff. Bill has recently moved from working full time in an accountancy firm to a part-time job. He works in the restaurant at weekends and evenings if they're short-staffed. He also does the accounts. Their teenage children work part time in the restaurant.

Blue Gum is a lifestyle as well as a business choice as Tania and Bill enjoy being in the hospitality industry.

## Jane Amos, natural therapist

Jane Amos is a natural therapist who offers massage, reflexology, reiki and Bowen therapy. Jane has been employed as a natural therapist for several years, but she started her own business two years ago. Jane is qualified to offer herbal and dietary services, but at this stage she has decided to concentrate more on body work.

Many of her clients are working mums, who juggle the competing demands of kids, husbands and work. They come to Jane to pamper themselves with 'time out' and to manage their stress levels better. Jane's services also attract women who are going through the menopause and want a better balance in their lives.

Being a keen sportsperson herself, Jane also has several clients, both men and women, who come to her for sports massage. These clients visit Jane before sporting events to improve their flexibility and after competing to improve the speed of recovery from injuries.

The services Jane offers are:

- **massage**—the use of touch and manipulative techniques on the body to relieve stress, tension and pain
- **reflexology**—the use of the hands to apply gentle pressure to the feet
- **reiki**—a form of hands-on healing
- **Bowen therapy**—the use of touch to target specific points of stress build-up in muscle groups.

# Chapter outlines

## Chapter 1   Planning

This chapter looks at the value of having a marketing strategy and an action plan. It also covers the need to regularly assess your business, evaluate the previous year, and analyse your own resistances.

## Chapter 2   What do you do?

Many people have difficulty knowing what to say when people ask them 'What do you do?' How you respond will depend on the situation. This chapter looks at five different ways of answering the question. Sometimes you'll just use a label, like 'I'm a writer', but at other times, the question is an opening for you to introduce your business in a way that attracts further questions.

## Chapter 3   Word of mouth and referrals

Word of mouth and referrals are a powerful and satisfying way to build your business as work comes your way through the strength of your reputation. Many businesses rely heavily on word of mouth and referrals to grow their business, but few understand how word of mouth works or have systems in place to increase the number of referrals they receive.

This chapter looks at how to enhance your word-of-mouth recognition and how to ask for referrals at all stages of your business relationships with clients or customers.

## Chapter 4   Networking

Many small businesses rely extensively on their existing networks to generate new business. Networking for small businesses often provides a support network as well as a source of referrals.

This chapter looks at the importance of thinking about what you want to achieve with networking, and how you can network more effectively by being well prepared and following up afterwards. It also includes some tips on how to work a room and avoid getting stuck in conversations.

## Chapter 5   Telemarketing

Many businesspeople hate picking up the phone and making cold calls, but once you start it's not as daunting as it first appears. One of the great advantages of telemarketing as a marketing tool is that you have an almost instant answer—prospects are either interested or they're not.

This chapter includes information on drawing up a target list, putting systems in place to record your calls, and what to say when you actually make the phone call. One of the keys to successful telemarketing is being a listener rather than delivering a pre-prepared spiel.

## Chapter 6   Public speaking

Public speaking is great promotion as your name appears in front of a wide range of people, both in the promotion for the event and at the actual event. If you're not very experienced at giving speeches, getting started may seem daunting. But many people find that, once they've overcome their nerves, they enjoy the thrill of public speaking.

This chapter looks at how to find speaking events, offers some tips on how to structure and deliver your speech, and gives some suggestions for developing an ongoing relationship with members of the audience.

## Chapter 7  Running seminars

Running seminars is a lot of work, but the results can be extremely rewarding. You can develop a deeper relationship with existing clients and customers and impress prospects with your willingness to share your intellectual property. Some businesses charge for seminars and others provide them free. There are pros and cons to both approaches.

This chapter covers the different types of seminars—traditional face-to-face seminars, teleseminars and webinars. It also includes some tips on how to promote the event.

## Chapter 8  More ways to talk up your business

There are many other creative ways of promoting your business, such as participating in street festivals, sponsoring local events, or attending trade shows. This chapter looks at some other ways of growing your business with the spoken word.

## Chapter 9  Grow your business from within

As you expand your business, you also need to pay attention to what's happening within your business. This chapter covers a wide range of internal business development topics including gaining new skills to keep up with your marketplace, managing your cash flow so you survive business ups and downs, and installing efficient processes and systems to make your business run more effectively.

# 1 Planning

When you're marketing your business you need to be clear about your direction or you risk being randomly pushed and pulled by prevailing currents. Sometimes this may result in unexpected bonuses, but more often it will lead to confusion and chaos. One minute you're a specialist in one thing and the next minute you're off on a different tangent.

Some people are resistant to planning as it seems too rigid and confining. It needn't be. You can dream your dreams and set your goals while still remaining flexible and open to opportunities that seem to come out of nowhere.

When you started your business, you may have written a business and marketing plan because people told you every business 'should' have one or maybe the bank wanted to see a copy before giving you a loan.

I know I didn't value my business and marketing plan until I'd been in business for a while. I used to read about things like

SWOT (strengths, weaknesses, opportunities and threats) analyses and USPs (unique selling propositions) and think 'What's the point? Let's just get on with it'. I now have a combined business and marketing plan, which I review annually—or more often if I need a boost of energy.

Having a plan helps you clarify your thinking around the following areas.

- What products and services do you currently offer and will you change any of these products or services in the coming year?
- Who are your current clients and customers and what new target markets would you like to reach in the coming year?
- Can you describe your USP (sometimes known as a Customer Value Proposition or CVP) without 'ums' and 'ahs'? In other words, what differentiates you from your competitors?
- Do you have a distinctive brand which runs consistently through your marketing material and all your processes, such as the way your staff answer the phone?
- What are your values and beliefs? Is your business in line with your values or beliefs?
- What marketing tools have been successful for you in the past and what marketing tools will you use this year?
- What's your budget for your marketing this year?
- What deadlines are you going to set for achieving your business goals?

If you don't have a business and marketing plan, take time out to write one. There's a chapter in *Promote Your Business* on writing a marketing plan and plenty of websites offer templates. If you do have a business and marketing plan, pull it out and re-evaluate it. A lot of your plan may still be relevant each time you look at it, but you'll have to fine-tune it and re-set your goals and objectives from time to time.

## Review your business

When you're writing or rewriting your marketing plan, review the current state of your business objectively. Look at your business with a critical eye and see whether you're satisfied with the current state of your business. Ask yourself:

- Is your business profitable enough?
- Is your business still fun or has it swallowed your life?
- Does your marketing material still accurately reflect your business?
- Is all your marketing material consistent with your branding?
- Have you got systems in place that make your business easier to run?
- Are there any areas you could outsource to make your business more efficient?

RESTAURANT

Tania James and Bill Johnson analysed their business and realised that on the whole they were satisfied, but that if they wanted to take time off, they needed to make their business more efficient so it could run without them. They decided to get a computerised booking system linked to their existing database.

> They also acknowledged that their teenage children, who had been helping at weekends, were no longer as willing to do so, so they needed to find some experienced casual workers.

## Do you have a niche market?

Many marketing experts recommend that you develop a 'niche' so you become known as an expert in your field. Your strength then lies in sticking to what you're good at and not deviating from it. Your niche could be either a particular product or service, or a specific target market. For example, a public speaker may find a niche market as an MC and give up doing other types of speaking so they become known solely for that skill. Or a public relations business may specialise in providing a wide range of marketing and communication services to clients in the healthcare industry.

Although I can see the merits of having a niche, I personally don't follow this advice as I offer writing, training and marketing services. One of the advantages of offering more than one product or service, or working with a wide market, is greater flexibility. Your business can change to take advantage of new opportunities or your changing interests.

## Say 'no' to unwanted work

Many small businesses find it hard to say 'no' to work. There's the fear that you may lose the client or customer to a competitor or that you'll get a reputation for being difficult to work with.

But sometimes you have to be ruthless. You have to say 'no' if you've got too much work on. At those times, you can often refer the work to a colleague and, more often than not, still retain the client.

You also have to say 'no' if you're serious about no longer doing work that doesn't fit with your business goals. If you say 'yes' to work you don't want to do because your workload is lean, you risk resenting the work and struggling to give it the quality attention it deserves. Better to sit out the lean period if you can afford to.

## Review your past year

Before you set or re-set your goals for the year ahead, review your past year. Analyse how you acquired new clients or customers and how much repeat business you attracted. If you don't have this information, maybe you can do a survey of past and current customers or clients.

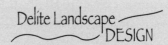

John Pettit's goals for the previous year were to increase profits by 10 per cent, develop a new balcony design service, and improve staff motivation. His seven-year goal is to sell or franchise the business.

That year he achieved a 7.5 per cent increase in profits; he successfully introduced his new balcony design service; and a customer survey indicated that overall, customers were pleased with Delite's customer service. Customers commented on the staff's helpfulness and knowledge of plants. The only negative remarks were that sometimes customers felt they waited too long for attention and that some popular plants sold out too early in the season.

> ### Blue Gum RESTAURANT
>
> Tania James and Bill Johnson's goals for the previous year included providing a quality dining experience, increasing profitability by 5 per cent, increasing the lunchtime trade, and enjoying themselves.
>
> Their profitability increased by 6.5 per cent; they increased their lunchtime trade by 4 per cent; introduced new dishes to the menu; and sent their chef on a weekend refresher course. They also introduced a new service—dial-a-dinner—which had not been one of their original goals. The idea came to Tania and Bill when they took time off because they were feeling flat and unmotivated.

This analysis will give you some understanding of which marketing tools are working for you. But remember that some marketing takes time to be effective and many businesses give up on marketing before it has a chance to work. Customers or clients often need to hear about your business several times before they feel comfortable dealing with you.

## Look at your own weaknesses and resistances

Have a look at what holds you back personally. Why don't you make those follow-up calls after a networking event? They only take a few minutes, yet so many of us put them off until it seems too late to make the call. Are there any internal emotional resistances you need to deal with or is it simply a time-management problem? If you have inner fears stopping you, face them and they won't seem as bad. If you're truly blocked, seek help from a friend, counsellor or business coach.

One technique you can use to look at your resistances is to write 'because' statements. For example, 'I put off telemarketing because . . .', 'I don't follow up after a networking breakfast because . . .', or 'I avoid giving speeches because . . .'.

Then confront the reasons you've given by finding evidence that contradicts these beliefs. If the reasons you've given are valid, then maybe that's not the right marketing tool for you. But more often the reasons will be excuses, and having identified them, you can find ways of overcoming them.

Looking at your weaknesses and resistances may also identify areas where you need further training or processes you could employ someone else to do. This aspect of promoting your business is covered in Chapter 9.

**Jane Amos**
NATURAL THERAPIST

**Belief:** 'I don't like marketing myself because I would prefer to grow my business through word of mouth.'
**Contrary evidence:** 'I don't get enough business through word of mouth.'

**Belief:** 'I hate making speeches because people may disagree with what I say.'
**Contrary evidence:** 'They may, but so what?' and 'I'm an expert in my field and can support what I say with evidence and experience.'

**Belief:** 'I don't like public speaking because I may forget my words.'
**Contrary evidence:** 'I didn't forget my words when I spoke at Rotary last month' and 'If I forget my words, I can always look at my notes.'

# Program yourself to win

Many successful business people prepare themselves for the sales process by creating the end results in their minds before they start. Some people do this through visualisation—they 'see' a picture in their head and watch themselves closing the deal and shaking the prospect's hand. Some 'feel' the outcome, imagining how they will feel when they're successful, and others 'hear' the words that accompany the sale. Whatever method you use, imagining an outcome before you start helps you believe success is possible.

When you do have a setback, pick yourself up again and just keep going. It's a bit like managing chronic pain, such as a backache. Detach yourself from your feelings and do as much on the bad days as the good, as you never know when you're going to be successful. At times though, still using the back-pain analogy, if the pain becomes acute rather than nagging, you may need to take time out to deal with the issues causing the pain, or attend to other, less stressful, parts of your business.

Regard all your rejections as valuable data. Our setbacks are usually our greatest teachers and you can use them to improve your sales skills and identify any problems with your products, services or marketing material.

For example, in one of my early training sessions, I expected to have a whiteboard or flipchart in the training room and arrived to find neither were available. I had planned to write the structure of the program on the board or flipchart before people arrived. I quickly wrote an additional slide for my PowerPoint presentation and was feeling so stressed that I made a typo, which was not a good start for a training session on writing.

I learnt two things from that experience: I now always ask what equipment is available instead of making assumptions, and I also incorporate the structure of the program in the participants' workbook. I've never been caught out like that again.

## Believe in your product or service

One of the best ways to build trust with your prospects is to truly believe in your own product or service. Then you'll believe that selling your product or service is something you do *for* somebody, rather than *to* somebody. This way you will be thinking about how your client or customer will benefit from your product or service, not just how much money you will make.

Zig Ziglar, an American author and speaker, says selling is essentially a transference of feeling. He tells the story in *Secrets of Closing the Sale* (1984, pp. 81–86) of when he was a successful cookware salesman and Bill, one of his associates, was 'starving to death'. Bill had been with the company for five years but didn't own its brand of cooking pots as there was always a more pressing use for money, such as car repairs and hospital expenses. So when Bill's prospects said they didn't think it was the right time to buy, he thought 'Yeah, I know exactly what you mean. That's the reason I don't have a set of the stuff myself.'

When Bill realised the impact of not owning the cookware on his sales, he bought a set of pots. Now he was able to sell with empathy, rather than sympathy, and the additional sales he made that week paid for his own set. Bill still understood how his prospects felt, but no longer felt the same way. The problem with sympathy is you get involved in the other person's problems and lose your objectivity.

>
> **Jane Amos**
> NATURAL THERAPIST
>
> Jane Amos is an ardent believer in the power of natural therapies for both prevention and treatment. She believes that:
>
> - reflexology clears blockages in the energy field, putting people in touch with the source before it manifests as disease
> - massage improves the body's circulation and removes tension from the mind and body
> - Bowen therapy puts the body back into physical integrity
> - reiki draws on universal healing energy.
>
> Because Jane believes in the value of her services, she finds it easy to convince her clients of the benefits of her therapies.

# Set your goals

Goals are big-picture aims, while objectives are more specific. For example, if one of my goals is to run marketing workshops for professional service organisations, one of my objectives might be to gain six new clients in the next financial year. Then I write 'to do' lists to help me reach those objectives.

Keep your list of goals short and simple. Ten is a good maximum number. Your goals don't have to be totally work-oriented—ideally, they should be balanced with personal aims, such as fitness and social goals. Once you've written your goals, put them in a prominent place where you can look at them regularly and review them when necessary. Australian real estate agent John McGrath (2003, pp. 35–36) laminates his goals and puts them up in the shower where he can see them every day.

I put mine on my paper stand by my computer underneath my 'to do' list.

As we all learn in different ways, some people prefer to put pictures of their goals on the wall, turn them into a collage, or stick them into a scrapbook. Someone I know has even changed the dial tone on her phone into a recording of positive affirmations which she hears every time she picks up the phone to make a phone call.

Whatever method you use, the more you imagine yourself achieving your goals, the more possible your dreams will seem.

John Pettit's goals for the year ahead are:

- increase profits by a further 10 per cent
- develop a strategy for selling or franchising two of Delite's branches in three years' time
- grow the balcony design side of the business
- continue to provide staff training to maintain Delite's high-quality customer service
- write a garden design book for city dwellers
- become recognised as a public speaker on 'gardening for the city dweller'
- gain a professional speaking qualification
- take a three-week overseas holiday in September to coincide with a gardening trade show in Europe
- run seminars for city gardeners and ask key staff to take a lead role in these seminars
- attend two networking events each month and encourage key staff to do the same.

## *Blue Gum* RESTAURANT

Tania James and Bill Johnson's goals are to:

- increase profitability by 4 per cent
- continue to build up the lunchtime trade
- increase the use of their function room
- attend at least one networking function a month
- introduce weekend cooking seminars in a country location
- give one free speech a month to community groups
- develop an incentive for referrals
- review the menu and wine list in July
- schedule a few days off every three months
- take time out for a massage once a week.

## Jane Amos NATURAL THERAPIST

Jane Amos's goals for the year ahead are to:

- earn more than $80 000 in gross profit
- provide quality service that attracts repeat business and word-of-mouth referrals
- move into training so patients learn how to help themselves
- make time for a monthly healing herself
- do at least one training course to keep up with new techniques
- grow the business through public speaking
- set up a website and start a monthly e-newsletter
- take a holiday at least every six months
- exercise regularly—walking, yoga, swimming and squash
- eat a balanced diet and restrict chocolate to special treats.

Not only will you start to create opportunities to realise your goals, but you will also develop greater confidence in your ability to achieve them and start noticing opportunities when they come your way.

## Write an action plan

Once you've set your goals, work out what you need to do to bridge the gap between where you are now and where you want to be. Your objectives, which will help you reach your goals, must be measurable, achievable and profitable.

When writing an action plan, you can either plan a series of actions that will lead to where you want to be, or set your end destination and plan backwards so you're clear about all the necessary steps you need to take. Whether you plan backwards or forwards, divide your plan into manageable steps with a time frame.

Remember that providing specialised products or services, or targeting a very specific market, makes your marketing easier. Few small businesses have the budget to do huge advertising campaigns or the newsworthiness to get unlimited media coverage. Marketing based on developing relationships, while more time-consuming than mass marketing, is generally more successful for small businesses.

**Jane Amos**
NATURAL THERAPIST

**Goal:** Grow the business through public speaking

| Target markets | Objectives | How | August to do |
|---|---|---|---|
| • Working mums<br>• Change of life women<br>• Sportspeople | • Gain six new clients a month<br>• Sell three gift vouchers a month | • Give two speeches a month, starting in August<br>• Put brochures and flyers in doctors' rooms, beauty salons and hairdressing salons<br>• Take part in a 'Pamper Yourself' seminar<br>• Set up a website and start an e-newsletter<br>• Make phone calls one morning a month<br>• Attend at least one networking function a week | **Speeches**<br>• Draw up a list of event organisers and spend 2 hours a week contacting them<br>• Do a public speaking course<br>• Join National Speakers and Toastmasters |

# 2 What do you do?

Many small business owners find it hard to answer that perennial question 'What do you do?' Sometimes it's out of shyness or modesty, but at other times it's because your business is complex and you don't know how to describe it simply without going into great detail. As a colleague put it, it's easier to say 'mother of two' than 'corporate governance'.

Yet, as we all know, first impressions count and it's not just the way you look and the clothes you wear, it's also the first words you utter. How you introduce yourself will often determine whether the other person wants to invest their time talking to you. Often you'll get it right intuitively, but sometimes you say too much and watch their eyes glaze over, or you mumble something incoherent and spend the next few minutes thinking about what you should have said instead.

The answer to 'What do you do?' is often referred to as your 'elevator pitch' or 'elevator statement' because your reply should take about the same amount of time as it takes to ride in an elevator. Elevator pitches are also known as sound bites, benefit statements or audio logos.

## General introduction tips

This chapter looks at different formulas for answering the question 'What do you do?' I trialled these methods with colleagues at a networking meeting and we agreed on the following.

- Your answer must be short—about 30 seconds. Any longer and your listener's attention will wander.
- The best answers avoid current buzz words or generic words, such as *empowerment, focus* and *communications*.
- Stories and details need to be memorable. One woman, talking about a hotel she owns, aroused our interest by telling us her hotel allows dogs.
- Sincerity is more important than having a word-perfect pitch. When people delivered rehearsed scripts, they sounded wooden, but when they talked naturally about their business, their enthusiasm shone through and they were interesting to listen to.
- Your answer is the beginning of a conversation, not a sales pitch. If you think about the person you're talking to rather than yourself, you take the pressure off delivering the perfect response.

## Do your homework

Before you start developing short, punchy introductions, take an objective view of your business from your own perspective. You need to clarify what you do and what you stand for before you can talk about your products or services from your customer's or client's point of view.

- Describe your business. Write or dictate into a tape recorder a long version of what your business does and then condense it to a sentence or two. You probably won't say these actual sentences, but doing this exercise will help clarify the main points you want to get across to your listener.
- What makes you an expert in your field? Have a look at your qualifications, skills and experience. Ask yourself: What have been some of my successes? Am I renowned for anything? What makes me an expert in my chosen field?
- What's your unique selling proposition (USP) or point of difference? For some small businesses it's easy to identify what makes them unique, but for others with products and services similar to those of thousands of other businesses, finding that point of difference is difficult. One way of overcoming this problem is to find a niche position in the marketplace. So a business coach may specialise in working with women, a trainer might work with professional services organisations, and a writer could specialise in writing annual reports and business plans. Another way is to look at your own personal attributes and interests.
- What inspires you about your business? Think about your vision for your business and your life. Does your vision still motivate you or do you need to rethink what you're doing and why? If your heart's in your business, you'll convey that to your listeners. It will come across in your tone of voice and your body language as well as your words.
- What value do you offer your clients or customers? Once you've looked at your business from your point of view, ask yourself what benefit or value your clients get as a result of using your product or service.
- Listen to what your customers and clients say. Ask people to describe your business and its service. Some people ask this

question when closing a sale, others include it in a survey or evaluation form, or you could just ask your friends and colleagues what they would say if somebody asked them what you did. Don't be surprised if your friends' answers are no reflection of what you actually do—just learn to articulate what you do more clearly.

### What I do—a self perspective

**Jane Amos**
NATURAL THERAPIST

I'm a natural therapist offering massage, reflexology, reiki and Bowen therapy. I have a Diploma in Natural Therapies and have continued to do professional practitioner training every year. I have a wealth of experience from working with some of the top practitioners, both here and overseas.

Even though I'm highly qualified and experienced, other therapists could say the same so it's hardly a USP (unique selling proposition). To differentiate myself, I've decided to specialise in three areas: working mums, change of life women and sportspeople. I've chosen these areas because they interest me personally. I'm a working mother, a keen sportsperson and I've watched my mother go through menopause.

While I don't see myself as a counsellor, I am often privileged to hear people's life stories. What I love about my business is watching people change as they deal with emotional issues which so often manifest in physical tension in the body. Sometimes people only come to me in a crisis and I never see them again. That's not as satisfying as the ongoing work, but I still enjoy seeing them walk out of my clinic in less pain.

I know I offer value to most of my clients. I have the occasional person I don't relate to, but they're the exception and I've learnt not to get upset about them. My treatments remove or reduce my clients' physical pain as well as releasing stress and tension. I pamper my clients so they walk out feeling relaxed and confident.

> I've asked a few regular clients how they view my treatments and I've received some glowing testimonials which I'll use on my website. Some clients aren't really interested in the specific techniques I use as it's the end result that matters. Others have definite preferences. Some like therapeutic massage because it's hands on and others prefer reiki because they don't have to take their clothes off.

## Types of introductions

You need different introductions for specific scenarios, such as for the phone or email, in social networking situations, for speeches and for those chance encounters with people you meet in everyday life. Sometimes, if your business has several aspects, you might decide to concentrate on one area that you think will interest your listener rather than overwhelm them by summarising everything you do.

### Labels

Businesspeople often introduce themselves with a label—'I'm an accountant' or 'I'm a management consultant'.

In social networking situations, the question 'What do you do?' is often just a courtesy and a label is appropriate as it's brief and doesn't impede the general flow of conversation.

John Pettit: 'I'm a landscape gardener.'

## *Blue Gum* RESTAURANT

Tania James or Bill Johnson: 'I own a restaurant.'

Jane Amos: 'I'm a natural therapist.'

Sometimes, however, a label is not helpful as the listeners may assume wrongly that they understand what accountants or management consultants do. If that's the case for your business, choose a more specific introduction that gives the listener an accurate idea of what you do.

### Think about benefits and solutions

It's often easier to describe *how* we do things than to talk about what *results* we achieve for our clients or customers. Yet talking about benefits and solutions is usually more powerful than talking about processes. Compare the following approaches:

> I work with clients who want to improve their proposal writing. I do this by providing training and also editing their proposals (*process*).

> I help companies win more tenders by improving the quality of their written proposals (*benefits*).

You can use the following formula to create your answer:

I help/assist/work with ..................................................
(*name of your target market*)
to ..................................................
(*name your solution*).

### Delite Landscape DESIGN

John Pettit: 'I help apartment dwellers create a garden on their balconies or patios.'

### 𝓑lue 𝓖um RESTAURANT

Tania James or Bill Johnson: 'Our restaurant helps busy people eat better by providing a dial-a-dinner service.'

###  Jane Amos NATURAL THERAPIST

Jane Amos: 'I help mothers look after their own wellbeing by giving them a relaxing, therapeutic massage.'

## Relate your answer to 'problems'

A similar benefits-oriented approach is to relate your solutions to problems your prospects or clients face. This approach demonstrates that you understand your customers' or clients' needs and have the ability to solve these problems. You're working *with* your clients or customers rather than imposing your ideas on them.

I help/assist/work with .................................................
(*name of your target market*)
who are struggling/having problems with
.................................................................................
(*name their problem*).

Use this approach with tact and caution: although some prospects might feel relieved that you understand their needs, others might feel defensive and not want to admit they have a problem. You may also choose another word instead of 'solution' as this word is often overused.

John Pettit: 'I help apartment dwellers who hate not having a garden create a paradise on their balcony.'

Tania James or Bill Johnson: 'Our restaurant helps busy people who are sick of eating junk take-aways to eat better by using our dial-a-dinner service.'

**Jane Amos**
NATURAL THERAPIST

Jane Amos: 'I help mothers who feel tired and stressed pamper themselves a little.'

You know how . . .

When you're in a situation where you're talking to someone who is genuinely interested in your response, you may choose to use a 'You know how/What I do' statement. This type of statement is particularly useful if most people will relate personally to what you do.

The first part begins with 'You know how . . .' then you follow up with 'What I do'. For example:

> You know how you sometimes struggle at work because your computer goes slow and you have to reboot it all the time? Well, we fix those problems for businesses.

This introduction is effective as you're stressing benefits from your listener's point of view rather than just talking all about yourself and how good you are. You're also demonstrating that

---

**Delite Landscape DESIGN**

John Pettit: 'You know how some people living in apartments with balconies really want a garden? What we do is create an attractive, easy-to-maintain balcony garden for them.'

---

***Blue Gum* RESTAURANT**

Tania James or Bill Johnson: 'You know how some people are too busy or too tired to cook but appreciate home-cooked food? Our restaurant offers a dial-a-dinner service so they can curl up in front of the television and enjoy a home-cooked meal.'

Jane Amos: 'You know how some mums get stressed trying to balance everything in their lives? I provide relaxing massages and other natural therapies, such as reiki, to help them keep their lives on track.'

you're an expert in your field and have empathy for your clients or customers. This technique is useful for people who don't like saying the word 'help' because it has connotations of being a 'do-gooder'.

Create visual pictures

Another powerful way of introducing yourself is to create a mental picture that your listener can visualise or imagine. This gives an emotional impact to your introduction. For example:

> Sally, imagine if you were losing all the tenders you pitched for because you couldn't express yourself clearly in writing. You'd need someone to help you. That's me. I help companies and individuals write winning proposals.

Tania James or Bill Johnson: 'Sue, imagine you've just come home from a long day at the office and you feel like curling up in front of the television with one of your favourite home-cooked meals, like shepherd's pie or an old-fashioned roast. Well, our restaurant delivers these home-cooked meals to your doorstep.'

# Following up

Often, when you've made your brief elevator statement, the other person will want to know more about your business and will ask further questions. This allows you to elaborate, but avoid the temptation to swamp them with boring details about *how* you do things.

Relate your response to your listener

One way of following up is to ask your listener where they work and relate your response to their industry or situation. For example, if you make office furniture, you could ask them where they work, what the office furniture is like in their office, and whether many people suffer from back pain. You could then explain the benefits of your ergonomic chairs.

RESTAURANT

Tania James: 'Our restaurant helps busy people eat better by providing a dial-a-dinner service.'
Other person: 'That sounds great. Tell me more about it.'
Tania James: 'You're obviously a busy person. Where do you work?'
Other person: 'I work in the financial services sector and I often work late. It would be great to order a decent meal rather than sending out for the same old take-aways.'
Tania James: 'Our menus are on our website and you can order online or over the phone. I'll give you my card.'

## Follow up with a story

Stories are another way of keeping your listener's interest and demonstrating the value of your products or services. You can tell a story, without using names, of a customer or client you worked with recently.

You need to keep your story brief—explain what the situation was before you worked with the client or customer, what you did for them (without going into much detail), and what happened as a result of your work. For example, a business coach

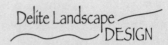

John Pettit: 'We recently worked with a client who had sold their family home in the suburbs, as the kids had all left home, and moved into a city apartment. They really missed their garden, especially their vegetable patch.

'We created a balcony garden for them that gave them greater privacy from their neighbours and we also showed them how to grow vegetables in containers. They're now growing mushrooms, potatoes, tomatoes, lettuces and herbs—all on their balcony.'

Jane Amos: 'I recently worked with a woman who was feeling very tired and had no energy. It was a classic case of the midwinter blues, but she couldn't afford to take time out, go to bed or have a holiday as she had three children under five, a part-time job and a mortgage.

'Using a combination of reflexology and Bowen therapy, I worked on her immune system and three weeks later she was full of energy and even considering standing for president of her local kindergarten.'

could tell the story of a client whose business was struggling to get new clients and how, as a result of the coaching, the client trebled their business within three months.

## Introducing yourself to a group

Often in networking groups, you'll be asked to say something about yourself in 60 seconds. There's an art to these introductions. Some people drone on and on and everyone else inwardly groans with embarrassment, and others say something as fast as possible to get it over and done with so they can sit down again.

In *Masters of Networking* (Misner and Morgan 2000, p. 199), Steve Lawson illustrates what a wasted opportunity self-effacing introductions are:

> I watched a travel agent stand in front of twenty-five business associates and say, 'I guess you all know what a travel agent does, so if you are going on holiday call me.' I could almost hear her audience thinking, Nope, can't take a vacation this week. How much more powerful and effective it would have been if the travel agent had said, 'Last week our agency bought a large block of Caribbean cruise tickets at a ridiculously low price. If you're talking to friends, clients or business associates, and they complain of being overworked and tired, tell them you know of a travel agency that has some unbelievable three, four or five-day cruises at amazingly low prices! Listen for two key phrases this week: "I'm tired," and "I'm overworked". When you hear those phrases, think of me.' By saying this she would have both educated her associates and got them looking for a specific kind of referral for her.

John Pettit: 'My business is Delite Landscape Design in Landscape Lane. We've just received our new-season camellias and have an outstanding range to choose from. There's a new miniature white camellia that's scented. It's exquisite.

'Our latest shipment of pots also arrived last week and they're selling at amazingly low prices.

'So if you hear anyone talking about gardening this week, think of me and tell them to get in quick before our camellias and pots sell out.'

## Answering the phone

Listen to the way you answer the phone. Does it sound in keeping with your brand? A common mistake—and one I sometimes make—is speaking too fast so the person is not sure they've reached the right number.

Most people usually say some form of greeting, such as 'hello', 'hi' or 'good morning', followed by their company name and their own name: 'Hello, Delite Landscape Design, John Pettit speaking.' Some businesses then add 'How can I help you?'

Say words that come naturally to you and practise the way you say them. Some people find it helps to smile as they answer the phone; others say that they sound more positive if they stand up when they're talking on the phone.

Also, listen to your voicemail. Is your message clear and easy to understand? If you leave a mobile phone number, consider saying it twice to give people time to write it down.

# Introducing yourself as a speaker

When you're public speaking, it's a good idea to present a brief profile to the person who's introducing you. Otherwise you may find they use material they've found somewhere that's either out of date or inaccurate. Most comperes will thank you for making

It is my pleasure to introduce to you John Pettit from Delite Landscape Design.

John is recognised as a leading expert in landscape design.

He has experience in designing and creating backyard gardens, large-scale commercial gardens, and more recently, balcony gardens for apartment dwellers.

John set up Delite Landscape Design 27 years ago and his company has branches in three cities. Over the years, Delite has won several design awards including the prestigious '*Gardens for Today* Garden of the Year Award' in March this year.

He has appeared on the popular TV program *Gardening for the 21st Century* and is a regular presenter on XYZ's radio talkback where he answers callers' gardening questions.

A family man, John's children have now all left home. He understands first hand the challenges and delights of gardening in the inner city as he and his wife sold their suburban home two years ago and moved into an apartment.

Tonight John is here to talk to us about how we can create attractive and manageable gardens in small spaces—indoors or on patios or balconies.

Could you please join me in welcoming John Pettit.

their job easier and will either read what you've said exactly or be even more fulsome in praising you. It's easier having someone else say glowing things about you than singing your own praises, which sounds boastful.

The importance of this was reinforced for me when I ran a workshop at a conference and the chairperson just said, 'And the next presenter is Mary Morel'.

# 3 Word of mouth and referrals

Word of mouth is the most powerful and satisfying way to attract new business. When prospects hear about your products or services through word of mouth, you're not starting a relationship with them from scratch—it's as if the prospect already knows you. Such prospects will often buy from you without shopping around as they've heard good things about your business and feel they can trust you.

Many small businesses take word of mouth for granted, yet it doesn't 'just happen'. A study by New Zealand Trade & Enterprise (2004) found that New Zealand businesses establishing themselves in the Australian market significantly underestimated how long it would take them to achieve a return on their initial start-up costs. The majority of businesses interviewed assumed it would take between three and six months to establish themselves in the Australian market. In fact, it took two-and-a-half to three years. They found their credentials counted for nothing and they had to establish themselves locally by slowly proving their worth.

Even when your business is established, you can't afford to rely on word of mouth entirely as it can be fickle and is not necessarily related to the quality of your product or service. You may well have superior products and services to those of your competitors, but if your competitors are better known than you, they may well attract more business. There's an unspoken assumption that high-profile businesses 'must' be good.

Nor is word of mouth consistent. Drop out of sight for a while because you're inundated with work and haven't got time to market, and it doesn't take long before word of mouth starts sending work to your competitors, rather than you.

So how does word of mouth work and how can you increase its effectiveness in your business?

# How word of mouth works

Two useful models when looking at how word of mouth works are the 's-curve' and 'tipping point' model, and the flywheel model.

### The s-curve and tipping point model

The way businesses grow is sometimes compared with the spread of disease and Malcolm Gladwell has popularised this concept in *The Tipping Point* (2000). He describes how both viral epidemics and the successful uptake of new ideas follow the same 's-curve'.

With both business and disease, there is a gestation period at first while the disease or idea germinates. Then a 'tipping point' is reached where the disease or idea either fizzles out or accelerates unexpectedly and rapidly up the steepest part of the s-curve. The s-curve can be illustrated by the uptake of new technologies such as the Internet, mobile phone and iPods.

Whether or not a business accelerates up the steep slope of the s-curve depends largely on word of mouth, but not everyone has the same degree of influence. If you want to run a successful word-of-mouth campaign, you need to reach the people who have the most influence. History is full of examples of innovations that failed to take off because they were not supported by people at the time.

Malcolm Gladwell's book was preceded by earlier work by Everett M. Rogers (2003, pp. 282–85) on the innovation adaptation curve. Rogers classifies adopters of innovation into categories based on the idea that some people are more open to innovation than others. His five categories are innovators, early adopters, early majority, late majority and laggards.

- **Innovators** (2.5%) are daring and rash and eager to try new ideas. They are able to cope with high degrees of uncertainty. They lead the change, but are often outside most people's social networks and their opinion may be suspect.
- **Early adopters** (13.5%) are next to try innovations. They are opinion leaders and when they adopt a new product or service, they spread the word to others through their networks. Their opinion and recommendation give the idea or product credibility and help decrease uncertainty.
- **Early majority** (34%) are those who follow willingly, but seldom lead. They adopt an innovation just before the average person.
- **Late majority** (34%) take more persuasion to be convinced. They approach innovations with scepticism and caution and are often finally motivated by peer pressure and economic necessity.

- **Laggards** (16%) are the last to adopt a new innovation. They tend to be suspicious of new ideas and prefer to use what they know. They will only try something new when they are convinced it will work and that they need it.

In *The Tipping Point*, Malcolm Gladwell (2000) says three psychological types are essential for spreading the word about your business: connectors, mavens and salespeople.

- **Connectors** know lots of people and have friendly, casual social connections with them. They manage to occupy many different subcultures and have the knack of bringing people together. They're like social glue and are great at spreading the message about new ideas.
- **Mavens** are information specialists and a source of reliable data. They often figure out how to get the best deals and are happy to tell you about it. They meet their own emotional needs by helping solve other people's problems. Their knowledge and social skills are invaluable in starting a word-of-mouth epidemic.
- **Salespeople** are persuasive. They're able to convince people with both their words and their body language. They're enthusiastic, charming and likeable. They draw you into their rhythm and dictate the terms of the interaction.

Marketers have successfully used opinion leaders for years. For example, this technique was successfully used to build demand for the *Trivial Pursuit* board game in the early 1980s. Originally an obscure Canadian board game, the marketing program for *Trivial Pursuit* consisted of sending toy buyers a series of provocative messages before the 1983 New York Toy Fair, giving the game to Hollywood stars whose names were mentioned in the questions, and staging tournaments in bars, restaurants, clubs and parks. Many stars wrote thank-you letters which were then used in promotions. Word of mouth did the rest.

### Using connectors

Tania James and Bill Johnson wanted to reach the human resources departments of large organisations to encourage them to book the restaurant's function room for their staff and clients. On Secretaries Day the restaurant put on a lunch for secretaries and support staff from HR divisions. The lunch was a set menu at a very reasonable price and they gave all the secretaries a free glass of champagne. They also gave every secretary a gift bag containing homemade chocolates and a pamphlet about their function room.

In the six months following this lunch, the bookings for the function room rose by 7 per cent. Each time a new booking was made, Tania sent the secretary responsible for the booking a thank-you card.

# Have a 'sticky' product

Knowing the right people is not enough to promote your business through word of mouth. Your product or service must also appeal to your audience with what Gladwell calls the 'stickiness factor' (2000, p. 19). It's easy to make assumptions about what works for your business, but you need to test these assumptions to find out what will make your product or service really 'sticky'. The creators of *Sesame Street* assumed they couldn't mix fantasy with reality and so originally there were no muppets in the street scenes. When they tested the show with children just before it went to air, they found the children were bored with the street scenes. So that's when Big Bird, Oscar the Grouch and Snuffleupagus were born.

> **Delite Landscape DESIGN**
>
> John Pettit assumed that older adults moving from houses into apartments would like the same sort of plants they were used to: camellias, roses and daffodils.
>
> He ran a few focus groups and showed slides of different balcony designs using a range of plants. He was surprised to find that many in the audience regarded moving into an apartment as a time to change every aspect of their lives and were taking a much more adventurous approach to gardening. They were interested in sculptural plants and green colour designs as opposed to colourful planting, and wanted low-maintenance plants that did not require much attention. They also wanted to experiment with different plants, such as succulents and bromeliads.

### The power of context

Sometimes it may not be the product or service itself, but the context you're promoting it in that makes a difference. Dr Paul Marsden, London School of Economics (2004), gives the example of Post-it Notes. In 1968, Dr Spence Silver, a research scientist for 3M, was trying to invent a new super-sticky glue. He failed, coming up with a super-weak glue instead. The failed invention was put to use six years later by another 3M employee, product development researcher, Art Fry, to mark pages in his hymnbook.

Initially, Post-it Notes didn't take off with consumers. The Post-it Notes failed in concept testing, prototype testing and even in a test launch. However, just before ditching the Post-it Notes, the company tried once more. This time they conducted a special research project, giving the Post-it Notes to highly connected secretaries of CEOs in large corporations. They sent large boxes of Post-it Notes to these 'connectors' and told them to share them with their colleagues and give feedback on any uses for them. The research project triggered an epidemic of word-of-mouth demand and Post-it Notes accelerated up the s-curve.

**Jane Amos**
NATURAL THERAPIST

Jane Amos was having difficulty encouraging local beauticians and hairdressers to display her brochures in a prominent place in their salons. They'd take the brochures, but when Jane next visited the brochures would be nowhere to be seen and Jane wasn't receiving any work from them.

So Jane invited about 30 leading local beauticians and hairdressers for a networking cocktail party at her clinic. Her clinic isn't large, so when 20 people turned up, it was a bit crowded, but that added to the intimacy of the event. During the evening, Jane offered anyone who wanted it a free five-minute head or shoulder massage. After that evening, she visited all the beauty salons and hair salons again with more pamphlets and this time many of them put the brochures in a prominent position.

Over the next six weeks, Jane received an average of two referrals a week from local beauticians or hairdressers.

## The flywheel model

Jim Collins in *Good to Great* (2001) uses the image of a huge, heavy flywheel to represent a company. A flywheel is a massive disc mounted horizontally on an axle. You need to get that flywheel to move as fast as possible, because momentum—mass × velocity—is what will generate superior economic results over time.

To get the flywheel moving requires a tremendous effort. You push with all your might, and finally you get the flywheel to inch forwards. After more sustained effort, you get the flywheel to complete an entire turn. You keep pushing, and the flywheel begins to move a bit faster. It takes a lot of work, but at last the flywheel makes a second rotation. You keep pushing steadily. The flywheel makes another turn. With each turn, it moves faster, and then at some point, you break through. The momentum of the heavy wheel kicks in your favour and the flywheel spins faster and faster, with its own weight propelling it. You don't stop pushing at this stage, but you no longer have to push as hard to keep the momentum going.

The growth of John Pettit's balcony design business has followed an s-curve. Initially, only one or two developers and real estate agents were interested in the concept and John almost gave up the idea. Then John started talking to Probus groups (associations of retired and semi-retired businesspeople) about gardening with an apartment lifestyle and at the same time started to run seminars around the theme of balcony gardening. He invited a reporter to one of his seminars, and a full-page article in a local paper boosted their profile. The combination of these three factors helped Delite's balcony design service tip up the s-curve.

Jane Amos thinks the flywheel model is more appropriate for her business than the s-curve as she has no desire for her business to accelerate dramatically beyond what she can personally handle. She plans to keep doing low-key marketing until she has as many clients as she wants. Even then, she knows she will have to continue marketing, as not all clients will become regulars and some will drop out.

# Ways of accelerating word-of-mouth business

Do a short survey of your current customers and clients and ask them how they heard about your products and services. This information will give you some idea of which marketing tools are working for you and what areas you need to concentrate on.

## Accelerate the buying process

One of the fastest ways of accelerating word-of-mouth conversion is to make the buying process easy for your prospects. Thanks to the Internet, the role of selling is changing. A DoubleClick (www.doubleclick.com) survey in 2004 found that consumers are less reliant on salespeople as more people are using the Internet to do research before making purchases, either online or over the phone, in shops, through banks, finance companies etc.

A Dieringer Research Group (www.thedrg.com) survey of 3000 US adults in June 2004 confirmed that researching and buying online is becoming increasingly popular (114.1 million adults have conducted product research online). This survey also found that consumers who buy online give a number of reasons why shopping online is superior to buying from other sources such as catalogues or retail outlets. These reasons include better time management, avoiding crowds, better prices and easier product searching.

Even if people just use the Internet for research, they are better informed about your business before they walk in the door or pick up the phone. You're often talking to people who already have some understanding of your business. This may be one of the reasons why you see fewer glossy brochures these days.

If you want people to research or buy online, you must make it easy for them to do so. Have a look at your business systems and see whether there are any roadblocks, bottlenecks, friction points or rough spots in your customer service. For example:

- Is all the information you provide on your website clear, relevant and up to date?
- If you don't have a website, is it time you got one?
- Do you offer a free trial so people can sample before they buy?
- Are your claims backed up by testimonials?
- Do you have generous guarantees?
- Is it easy to buy your products online?

### Blue Gum RESTAURANT

When Tania James and Bill Johnson introduced their dial-a-dinner service, the menus were on the Internet, but customers had to phone them to order a meal. Now Tania and James have introduced an online buying system. People can order and pay online and they also receive an estimated time of delivery. This has speeded up the buying process and also meant that one of their staff is free from answering the phone and taking orders.

## Spend 15 minutes a day staying in touch with people

One way of building word-of-mouth marketing is to keep in touch with your customers, clients and prospects at least every three months. Some people allocate 15–30 minutes a day to contacting people. Sometimes, you may not be in the mood to contact people every day or may have pressing deadlines that take precedence. Instead of giving up completely, why not allocate a longer period, such as a couple of hours or one morning at least once a month, to make calls, write cards and send emails?

During a treatment session, Jane Amos and her client, Clare, a woman with a new baby, discussed vitamins. Clare said she often felt overwhelmed in health food shops by the huge array of vitamins to choose from.

A week later, Jane came across an article on vitamins, which talked about the vitamin supplements that were most appropriate for mothers with small children. So she rang Clare:

'Hi Clare, I just came across an article about vitamins for new mothers and thought you might be interested in it. Would you like me to fax you a copy?'

Involve your staff

Involve your staff in your business so they talk positively about your products and services to their friends, family and colleagues. Tell them about your plans for the business, keep them informed about what's happening, and ask them for their suggestions. Share stories and anecdotes about the business and positive customer feedback that reflect on their service. If you have distributors or salespeople, encourage them to use or try the product themselves so they can speak about it positively from personal experience. For example, a biscuit manufacturer could give all his reps and distributors free cookies and encourage them to give free samples to their customers too.

Delite has fortnightly staff meetings over breakfast before the shops open. During these breakfasts, staff share good and bad customer stories.

John Pettit also offers his staff a generous discount on all the products in the store as most of them are keen gardeners. He figures the more his staff know about plants, the more information they will be able to share with his customers.

## Treat your first and special customers exceptionally well

When you start your business or when you introduce a new service or product, treat your first or special customers or clients exceptionally well—even if you have to subsidise this or give away things. Your exceptional service and generosity will accelerate positive word of mouth. For example, one new advertising company offered prospects a free TV advertisement in exchange for the chance to pitch for their future work if the ad was successful.

Another idea is to hold a special show or sale for preferred customers and allow them to bring a friend. For example, a women's clothes store holds fashion shows for select guests and their friends and allows them to shop at a discount after the show. Another store invites its special customers to shop the day before its sales start and offers them an additional 10 per cent off the sale prices.

Or you could introduce a loyalty program that entitles customers and clients to discounts or free gifts after a certain number of purchases. Many book stores and cafés use such loyalty programs.

John Pettit opened his nurseries after hours for a party and special sale before Christmas for Delite's priority customers and their guests. Delite provided drinks and nibbles, and entertainment for the children while the parents shopped.

Blue Gum Restaurant throws a Christmas party for their special guests and their friends. They have a set menu and ask the guests to pay a fixed amount, all of which goes to charity. They also ask guests to each bring a present under $10 for another guest. These presents go under the Christmas tree and the chef comes out of the kitchen after he's finished cooking and hands them out.

### Jane Amos
### NATURAL THERAPIST

Jane Amos gives all her regular clients a free half-hour session after ten sessions.

## Provide good after-service

Too often in small business, people do the job or sell the product, collect the money and move on. They treat payment as the end of the exchange and don't think about the lifetime value of that customer or client.

Often, what stays in people's minds about good service are the little things or the follow-up. When was the last time any of your suppliers or service providers contacted you? Imagine a restaurant ringing and asking if you enjoyed your meal, or even your garage emailing you to let you know your car is due for a service.

The way you follow up will depend on the nature of your business and whether you want repeat business or referrals. If you've done a one-off job for a client or customer, a thank-you card or phone call may be appropriate. Or you could include a small gift, such as chocolates, with the invoice. With ongoing clients, you will develop a stronger relationship if you contact them regularly to show an interest in their business and ask how your products and services are performing.

John Pettit makes a point of personally ringing all customers a month after Delite has installed their balcony garden. He has a casual chat and asks how they are enjoying their new balcony and if there are any problems. He'll answer any questions, offer to send more information and assure them they can contact him at any time in the future if they have problems.

Recent clients are Mr and Mrs Allison, who sold their large house and garden in the suburbs for an inner-city apartment when their last child left home.

John Pettit: How are you enjoying your new balcony garden?
Mrs Allison: We're loving it. It's giving us so much privacy from the neighbours.
John Pettit: Are all the plants thriving?
Mrs Allison: Now you mention it, there is one plant I'm a bit concerned about. A few of its leaves have turned yellow . . .

## Word of mouth and referrals 45

### *Blue Gum* RESTAURANT

Tania James rings corporate clients after they've held functions in the restaurant to find out whether they enjoyed their evening. An insurance company regularly holds its Christmas board dinner at the restaurant and Tania always rings Sue Smith, the human resources manager, the next day.

Tania: Hi Sue, I'm just ringing to say that once again we enjoyed having your board members at the restaurant last night. And I must say, I'm delighted to see you've now got more women on board! Seriously, though, I just wanted to make sure that everything went well from your point of view.
Sue: I'm pleased we've now got more women on the board too. I've had good feedback from last night. Everyone seemed to really enjoy themselves.
Tania: How was the menu? . . .

### Jane Amos
NATURAL THERAPIST

Jane Amos often calls clients after sporting events or games to ask how they got on and how their body feels. These calls sometimes prompt clients to come in for another appointment. For example, Jane heard that a client, John, had won a major marathon, so she rang him.

'Congratulations, John, you must be feeling so pleased with yourself. Do you think the massage you had beforehand made any difference? It did? That's great. You'd like to make an appointment to help you unwind? Good idea, what time suits you?'

### Use unconventional methods to get attention

One conference speaker sends Christmas cards at different times of the year so they stand out from all the other cards clients receive at Christmas. This speaker sends his cards when his clients are starting to plan their conferences for the following year.

### Acknowledge your supporters

Acknowledge people who make your business work—your clients or customers, suppliers, vendors, community supporters, family, colleagues and even your competitors. Make sure that the people in your life realise they contribute to the work that you do.

'Thank you' are two words that are much under-rated and can make a big difference to the way people feel about you and your business. Send thank-you cards, thank people personally, or invite your clients or customers to your office parties.

## Ways to increase your referrals

Referrals are great for your business and good for your ego. A single recommendation is often sufficient to convince a prospect to buy your product or service. Being unpaid, referrals are viewed with less scepticism than paid promotions.

A referral can be an indirect introduction, where your contact gives you a person's name and says you can use their name when you contact the person. Or your contact may go one step further and talk to the prospect about your products or services, paving the way for you to contact them or for the prospect to contact you. And sometimes your contact may even personally introduce you to the prospect.

People have different motivations for making referrals. Some do it just because they like being helpful, while others make referrals in exchange for a return favour, a percentage of the sale or a gift. In my experience, referrals don't usually work as cleanly as 'swaps'. More often you'll make a referral to a colleague for no return and then receive a referral from someone else.

When asking for a referral, open-ended questions generally get the best results. A closed question, such as 'Do you know of anyone . . . ?' can too easily lead to a 'no' answer and that's the end of the conversation. Instead you could say: 'I'd like to work with more people like you. Who do you know who . . . ?' Or 'I'm expanding my business and I'd like your help. Who do you know who . . . ?' or 'I'm starting to specialise in . . . Who do you know who . . . ?'

## Become a referrer yourself

If you want to be on the receiving end of referrals, become a referrer yourself. Take a few of your colleagues' and clients' business cards to hand out to people you meet. You'll find that it's easier than you think to link people with similar interests and business objectives.

## Ask your clients and customers for referrals

Many small businesses feel reticent about asking for referrals. Some of the reasons given are: 'It seems pushy', 'It makes me appear desperate for work' or 'I don't know them well enough to ask for referrals'. But if you don't ask for a referral, the answer is always 'no', and if you make a habit of asking, you won't feel needy—it will just be a routine question.

Many of your clients or customers will be happy to give a referral, but wouldn't necessarily think of it unless you ask. Make it an ingrained habit to ask all your clients or customers for referrals at all stages of your business relationship, not just when you've satisfactorily completed a job or are looking for more work.

At the beginning of your relationship with your client or customer, you can explain that your business grows mainly through referrals and say you'd appreciate referrals if they're happy with your performance and the results. Some people may give you names or referrals immediately, while others will wait until the end. But by mentioning it at the beginning, you've seeded the idea. When the project is complete, remember to ask again and give them some business cards to give to colleagues.

Sometimes it may not seem appropriate to ask for a referral at the time, but that doesn't mean you can't ask at all. You can ask later when you make a follow-up phone call.

If there are key people in your industry that you haven't met but wish to approach, ask your client or customer if they know them. If they do and are willing to let you use their name as an introduction, your cold call has just become easier.

Whenever a client or customer gives you a name, ask them for information about that person and their business and do your own research as well. The more you know about them, the easier your conversations will be.

When John Pettit rings clients to make sure they are happy with their balcony gardens, he also asks them for referrals. So when he rang Mrs Allison and asked how she was enjoying the garden, he gave her advice on how to cure the yellow leaves on one of the plants and then said:

'We're expanding the balcony design side of our business. Who do you know who would enjoy a balcony garden?'

## Blue Gum RESTAURANT

When Tania James rings her corporate clients after they have held functions at the restaurant, after she has asked them how they enjoyed the evening, she also asks them for referrals. So, when Tania rang Sue Smith, human resources manager of an insurance company, whose board had recently dined at Blue Gum, she said:

'Sue, we're planning to build the corporate event side of our business this year. What other companies can you think of that might be interested in our services?'

## Jane Amos NATURAL THERAPIST

Jane Amos approaches doctors' receptionists in her area and offers them a free head and shoulder massage so they can recommend her services from first-hand experience. Once they have had a massage, she says:

'I'm glad you found that relaxing. Would you mind putting my brochures in your waiting room and mentioning my services to your patients? Thanks.'

## Inform your clients or customers about other products or services

Many small businesses offer a wide range of products and services or have more than one target group. Find a way of informing your client or customer about your full range of products or services or other areas of interest. For example, if you work in real estate, and have helped a family buy a house, you might tell them that as well as helping families you like working with older people who are moving into apartments or smaller houses.

## Work with your colleagues and competitors

You may have areas of specialisation that you do better than your colleagues and competitors and vice versa, so you can refer work to a colleague or competitor in a number of ways.

### SUBCONTRACTING
You can subcontract a competitor for a particular job if you take on a large contract you need help with. One of the advantages of subcontracting is that you still have the prime relationship with your client or customer.

### JOINT VENTURES
Another option is to create a temporary joint venture in which you are an equal partner. This may work well if you want to break into a new market as you can share the marketing costs and time.

Or you could form an informal alliance with a business with complementary services. For example, a writer and designer could offer a complete service, a florist and hairdresser could offer a bridal package, or a real estate agent could partner with a local pizza takeaway to offer residents a free pizza when they move into their new home.

### PAY A PERCENTAGE OR DO IT FOR NOTHING
Some businesses pay colleagues and competitors a commission for referring work to them. Often, this will be a percentage of the first order or a percentage of all work they receive for a period of time, such as a year. The commission is usually between 10 and 20 per cent.

Alternatively, you can make referrals to colleagues or competitors for nothing, based on the premise that 'what goes around comes around' and you'll receive referrals from other people in exchange.

Experiment and find what method you feel most comfortable with.

SEND AN ENDORSED LETTER

Find someone who serves the same clients but is not in direct competition with you. Ask this associate to write a letter about you on their letterhead with a special offer for your services. You could write the letter for them and pay the postage.

Jane Amos asked a beauty therapist she knew to write a letter about her services to her client base. The letter read:

> As a woman who appreciates the value of looking after herself, I thought you might be interested to learn about Jane Amos, a natural therapist, who offers the most relaxing massage I've ever had.
>
> So next time you're feeling a bit run down, or just want to treat yourself, why not make a day of it and have a massage as well as a facial? You'll feel fabulous.
>
> Jane's offering an extra half-hour for free with your first session if you take this letter in with you. I'm enclosing a brochure to give you more information about what she does.

## Give a gift as an incentive

Give people a gift in exchange for recommending your product or service. It doesn't have to be huge, just a token of your appreciation, such as chocolates or movie tickets. It's also a nice gesture to send people a small thank-you gift if they refer a client to you—whether or not you asked for the referral.

### Start an affiliate program

An affiliate program is another term for a reseller or third-party distributor. Affiliates resell products or services and receive a percentage of the profits. Affiliates join this program if they don't have the time or desire to create their own products or to add more products to their own existing product mix. Being an affiliate opens up another revenue stream for everyone involved. Before signing up, affiliates are often given a free sample to get an indication of the quality of the product they'd be selling.

---

*Blue Gum*
RESTAURANT

Blue Gum Restaurant has an affiliate program for its dial-a-dinner service. The local restaurants in the affiliate program order meals from Blue Gum Restaurant but market the service as their own, using mutually agreed branding and marketing material. Some restaurants anticipate demand and order meals in advance, other restaurants place orders on demand.

# 4 Networking

Networking is a powerful marketing tool for small businesses as it's a low-key way of developing relationships with colleagues and prospects. The mistake that many people make with networking is treating it just as socialising, rather than as a marketing exercise. To gain maximum benefits from networking, you need to regard it primarily as work, not as a brief escape from work.

It takes time to build worthwhile relationships through networking. Walk into any room with a new group of people and, no matter how friendly they are, you feel an outsider. Occasionally you may meet someone you immediately connect with, but more often you'll have to attend several events before you start to feel you belong to the group.

The more visible you are in a group, the more accepted you will be. The more involved you are in each group, the stronger and deeper the relationships you'll build and the more willing people will be to do business with you or pass on leads and referrals. One way to become more involved is to join the organising committee of a group. Then you'll start playing a host role, rather than standing and waiting for people to talk to you.

Your networking relationships become profitable when you feel you're benefiting from the relationship, for instance by acquiring new business, receiving support from colleagues or gaining new knowledge.

## What do you want from networking?

Think about what you want to achieve from networking. There are several different reasons for networking, including meeting new people—prospects or colleagues—and gaining new knowledge or skills.

### Meet prospects

Networking with prospects is a way of meeting people who are hard to reach using other marketing methods. For example, some companies receive so much direct mail or so many cold calls that they don't pay much attention to them. It's hard to break through the clutter.

In networking situations, prospects will treat you as an equal so avoid the temptation to use networking for your sales pitch. Save promoting your business for your follow-up. Once you've talked to a prospect, they're more likely to take your phone call, respond to your email or read your material instead of binning it.

### Share ideas and experiences

Many people who work in relative isolation find that networking gives them a support group. Sometimes it's difficult to talk to friends and family about your business as they don't understand the issues. At networking functions, you can share information, ideas and experiences with colleagues or other businesspeople. Some of your competitors or colleagues may even become friends or business associates. Even if the people you meet don't become friends or clients, they may become ambassadors for your business, making referrals on your behalf or giving you names of useful contacts.

### Find out what your competitors are doing

Networking is an easy way of keeping up with what your competitors are doing. Your competitors will talk more freely in social situations than at other times and often the guest speaker will be a person from your field. When you meet new competitors, you can research their websites afterwards to see what they're doing and if there are any ideas you can use.

### Educate yourself

Many networking events are also educational so as well as chatting to people, you can gain information or learn new skills. Hearing a guest speaker or attending a workshop may challenge your thinking or give you ideas for your business. You'll also keep up with some of the latest thinking in your field, including the current 'buzz words' that clients and customers are using.

### Be visible in your community

Visibility and credibility go hand in hand. The more visible you are in the community (provided you're regarded in a positive light, of course), the more credibility you'll have. There's an unspoken assumption that you must be good. So the more networking events you attend, the higher your community profile will be and the more business you will attract.

John Pettit attends networking functions to:

- maintain his profile with developers and business leaders
- mix with colleagues to keep up with the latest design trends
- listen to guest speakers who make him think about his approach to his work.

Tania James and Bill Johnson don't see networking as a prime source of business, but are often pleasantly surprised by the number of people they meet who later come to the restaurant. They network to:

- meet and talk with other businesspeople
- mix with other people in their industry to keep abreast of the latest trends and get a feel for how their competitors are doing.

**Jane Amos**
NATURAL
THERAPIST

Jane Amos regards networking as one of the main ways of growing her business, as people are unlikely to come to her for treatment unless they have met her or heard about her from others. She networks to:

- meet people who need her services or will recommend her
- raise her profile in the community.

# Choose your networking groups and events

There are three types of networking events for small businesses: events your prospects attend, events where you mix with people in your own industry, and functions that attract other small businesses.

There are a wide variety of networking groups to choose from. Some functions are purely social, but many have an educational component, often with a guest speaker. Sometimes you may be attracted to an event because of the quality of the guest speaker or the topic. At other times, the topic may not interest you, but if it is a networking group you value, go anyway, as the more regularly you attend events, the deeper the relationships you'll build. And the 'mundane' topic may turn out to be riveting!

If you're new to networking, you could start by attending functions of your professional association, local chamber of commerce, business enterprise groups and SWAP (Salespeople With A Purpose) groups. You can usually attend functions as a visitor before making a decision about whether or not to join a group.

How important networking is in your overall marketing plan will determine how many functions, and the sorts of functions, you attend. Your networking calendar needs to be balanced against your work commitments and budget. While most networking events aren't very expensive, the dollars can add up if you attend several functions a week.

I personally try to attend at least two networking events a month—one which colleagues attend and one which attracts potential clients. If something else catches my attention and I have time, I'll attend that too. More serious networkers attend two or more networking functions a week.

### Delite Landscape DESIGN

John Pettit enjoys networking but because he's busy he's decided to concentrate on two groups and attend as many of their meetings as he can.

- *Nursery and Garden Industry Association*—John is on the committee of his state branch. He regularly attends the monthly meetings and always goes to the annual national conference. John attends these meetings to keep up with current trends and to socialise with his colleagues.
- *Local Chamber of Commerce*—John attends local Chamber of Commerce events to find out what's happening in the community, maintain a high profile, and gain new business.

### Blue Gum RESTAURANT

Tania James and Bill Johnson don't have a lot of time for networking, but enjoy it as it gives them a different perspective on their business.

- *Networking breakfasts*—Tania James and Bill Johnson find networking breakfasts the most convenient time for them. Tania belongs to a women's business network group that meets monthly. It's a small intimate group and the women take it in turns to facilitate it and lead a discussion on wide-ranging topics, including public relations, dealing with staff and coping with your computer. Bill attends a weekly SWAP meeting in the city. He enjoys meeting up with friends, but also tries to talk to guests so he meets new people.
- *Restaurant Association:* Tania and Bill try to attend about three association functions a year to meet up with colleagues and keep up with what's happening in the industry. They particularly enjoy the wine-tasting evenings.

**Jane Amos**
NATURAL THERAPIST

As networking is one of Jane Amos's main ways of gaining new business, she tries to attend at least one networking event each week.

- *Natural Therapies Association*—Jane is a member of her local branch of the National Natural Therapies Association. The association has monthly meetings with guest speakers. These meetings keep Jane abreast of what's happening in natural therapies and she enjoys socialising with fellow therapists.
- *Women's Business Network*—Jane belongs to a women's business network group where she meets potential clients and talks to friends and colleagues.
- *National Speakers Association*—Jane has recently joined the local chapter of the National Speakers Association as she wants to develop her public speaking skills.
- *SWAP*—Jane goes to SWAP meetings to meet other businesspeople and gain referrals.
- *Business Referral Network*—Jane goes to her local fortnightly Business Referral Network meetings to give and gain referrals.

# Reasons why people fail at networking

Although networking is an effective and relatively cheap form of marketing, many people fail to get as much benefit from it as they could. If you've planned and budgeted for networking, you want to get a return on your investment. To get the most out of each networking event, you need to avoid some of the common errors that many novice networkers make.

### They treat networking as a social occasion, not a marketing exercise

Many people fail to benefit from networking because they treat networking as socialising, rather than marketing. They turn up late, talk to a few people and leave early. You may have a good time when networking, but more often than not you'll leave feeling as though you've wasted your time and money. Often, you'll collect business cards which you throw on the mounting pile of business cards gathering dust on your desk. Weeks—or months—later when you sort these cards, you have no idea who half the people are or where you met them, so the cards go in the bin. Sound familiar?

### They talk to the same people each time

Many people regularly turn up at networking events and talk to the same people each time. They may get to know these people better, but they're not enlarging their circle of acquaintances and so are limiting their networking opportunities.

### They fail to follow up

Many people, when they first start networking, neglect to follow up the people they've met between networking events. When you make time to follow up between events—even just an email or phone call—people remember you from one meeting to the next, and you don't have to spend time re-establishing relationships.

### They go for quantity, not quality

Some people make the mistake of treating networking as a numbers game and try to accumulate as many business cards as they can. Yet the main purpose of networking is to make meaningful contacts for your business, so it's the quality of the contacts you make, not the number of people you meet, that counts. It's better to have a few in-depth conversations than flit around the room touching base with several people who probably won't remember you later.

They give up too soon

Another mistake is to write off a networking group or event without giving it a chance. It's tempting if an event is not quite what you expect, or if you don't know anyone, to stand in a corner and judge rather than throw yourself into meeting new people. On such occasions, you may find yourself wanting to leave early, but remember it's usually better to talk to at least one new person or renew an acquaintance than leave early in a bad mood and never go back. Not every event is going to live up to your expectations, but you can usually salvage something if you make an effort to talk to people.

# Prepare for networking events

Once you've set your broad goals for networking, you also need to consider what you want to get out of each event. You may decide how many people you want to meet—though remember that talking to a few people in depth is better than talking to several superficially. Or there may be specific people you want to meet, so you'd like someone to introduce you to them. For example, when I first joined National Speakers, a friend introduced me to a marketing expert I wanted to meet.

## Plan your introductions

Think about what you will say when someone says 'What do you do?' Your response will vary depending on the situation, but whatever you say, your main aim in networking is to connect with the person and have a conversation, rather than tell them all about yourself (see Chapter 2).

People are more likely to remember you if they enjoy having a conversation with you than if you spend all the time merely talking about yourself. If you're enjoying the conversation, then swapping business cards at the end will be a natural thing to do.

## Check you have your business cards

It sounds obvious to take a good supply of business cards to networking events, but I know I'm not the only person who's arrived at an event and realised I've left my cards behind. So check before you leave that you've got your business cards and make sure you've got plenty of them.

Often, the main purpose of giving someone a business card is to receive theirs in exchange. Once you have their contact details, you can take the initiative and follow up. So even if you don't have your cards with you, collect other people's cards and if they want your details in exchange, write them on a piece of paper. It's not ideal, but it's better than not exchanging contact details at all.

Your business card must be in keeping with your brand and clearly state your name, company name and contact details. Think about your target audience when having your cards designed and, unless your audience comprises only young people, make your font large enough for most people to read comfortably. I've seen lots of stunning-looking cards that you need strong reading glasses or a magnifying glass to read.

Some people keep the same design for their business cards for years and others change their cards every six months so they have an excuse to give people their business cards again.

## Develop a database and filing system

Develop a way of managing the cards you collect so you can find them again and also remember who the person is. You may not want to add everyone to your database, but you still need to keep their cards and file them in such a way that they mean something to you later. Many people write the date they met the person on the card, where they met them, and a note or two about them. For example, 'met at XYZ, 6 July 05', 'wore a bright blue shirt' or 'likes go-cart racing'.

I use this method, which I learnt at a workshop run by networking expert Robyn Henderson (www.networking-towin.com.au). It's one of the reasons I recommend keeping your business cards simple. Cards with lots of information on both sides are difficult to write on, as are shiny cards, or cards with black or highly coloured backgrounds.

File your business cards in a way that suits you. Card holders are relatively inexpensive and you can allocate one for each networking group. Or, if networking is one of your major marketing methods, you could enter everyone in your electronic database. I only transfer the names of people I develop an ongoing relationship with to my computer database as this is a method which suits me. The advantage of putting people in your computer database is that you can record details of every phone call, email and meeting so you have a history of your relationship.

Whatever method you use, it's a good idea to glance at the names before you go to the next networking event to refresh your memory and remind yourself of details you can use to continue a conversation.

## At the event itself

Be an active participant at all meetings. Talk to new people, introduce yourself to the speaker, before or after their speech, and ask questions in question time.

### Take the initiative

Arrive early at each event so you can make the most of your networking time. Being early also puts you at an advantage as you can adapt to your surroundings and watch other people arrive. Speakers and event organisers usually arrive early, so you may be able to talk to them or even offer to help. Having a job to do will make you feel more involved and part of the event. It will also help you meet more people.

Many of you have probably had the experience of entering a room where everyone is talking and you're the only one standing alone. You try to break into a group by hovering at the edge and everyone ignores you. You end up leaving as soon as you politely can or spend all evening talking to one person you can't get away from.

When you enter a room, enter with confidence, then pause and look around for a moment. See if there's anyone in the room you'd like to talk to or, if you have the courage, you can stand on your own and wait for people to join you. It's often easiest to join a group of three people or more, rather than two people who may be engaged in a personal conversation.

Learn to take the initiative. Pretend you're the host and make other people feel comfortable. Approach someone you haven't met before and introduce yourself. Talk to someone who's standing by themselves and introduce them to people you know. Include people that hover at the edge of your group and, if you're all seated at a table, be the one who does the introductions.

When people are seated—during speeches and meals—try to sit next to people you don't know. Once you've made your choice, don't look around the room and think 'I wish I was sitting over there instead of here'. Instead, find out what you and the person sitting next to you have in common.

Taking the initiative comes easier for some people than others. If you're new to a group and shy about introducing yourself to others, you could ask someone in the group to introduce you to some of the people they know. Most people will be happy to do this for you.

If you don't find networking comes naturally, think about joining a business referral or networking group to overcome your shyness. In many of these groups, each participant has to give a 60-second spiel about themselves and their business. Preparing and delivering this brief introduction will give you the confidence to be more outgoing in groups. See Chapter 2 for suggestions on how to introduce yourself to a group.

**Jane Amos**
NATURAL THERAPIST

When Jane Amos attended a local networking breakfast she found herself at a table with a group of people who didn't know each other. 'Hi,' she said. 'I don't believe everyone at this table knows each other. Why don't we go round the table and introduce ourselves? I'm Jane Amos, a natural therapist.'

### Name tags

Name tags help with those embarrassing situations when you can't remember someone's name. If that does happen and the person isn't wearing a name tag, it's often easier to admit straight away you've had a mental block about their name, than not saying anything and then being too embarrassed to ask their name to introduce them to other people.

Some people who network frequently have their own personal name tag custom made and wear it at all networking functions. Such name tags look professional and are often a good talking point.

You may like to wear your name tag on your right-hand side as, when you extend your hand for a handshake, the other person's eyes automatically go to your right-hand side.

> *Delite Landscape DESIGN*
>
> John Pettit has had his own name tag created in the shape of a pot plant. His name is in the plant and the company name in the pot. He's also created similar name tags for all his staff and they wear them when working in the shops.

### First impressions count

First impressions count, so find out about the dress code beforehand. Most networking events are 'smart casual', but it's always better to check than feel uncomfortable because you're wrongly dressed.

It's easy to come across as aloof and unfriendly, when in reality you're shy or reserved, so try to overcome your natural reticence about meeting new people and smile. Most people will respond to a smile. And remember, you won't be the only person who's nervous.

## Make small talk

The first 60 seconds of a conversation with someone you don't know are the most difficult. One way of overcoming this impasse is to think about conversation starters on your way to the event, though remember that the aim of small talk is just to break the ice, not exchange information of great value or depth.

For example, you could talk about an item in the news or make a comment on the event, such as the room, traffic or parking. Although your remark may be trivial, it will break the ice. Be positive rather than negative, as negative remarks can make you sound like a moaner.

Another common starting point is to ask a question, such as 'What did you do at the weekend?' or 'How long have you been coming to these events?' If you ask a question, make it open-ended to avoid a 'yes/no' answer that might leave you wondering what to say next.

Avoid the starter 'I don't think we've met before' in case you have. If you're meeting a lot of people, you can sometimes not recall someone immediately and people are not going to be impressed if you can't remember them.

Small talk, while often pleasant, is not going to lead to a lasting relationship unless you discover common ground. It might be a shared interest or you may both live in the same suburb. Sometimes this connection happens immediately, while at other times you have to talk to someone several times before you start to have an in-depth conversation.

## Be a good listener

Good networkers are usually good listeners who genuinely want to hear what the other person has to say. They're not looking around the room during the conversation to see who else they'd rather talk to. All their attention is on the person they're talking to.

After the introductions, invest most of the conversation in asking the other person questions about themselves and their business. They'll find you more interesting if you're a good listener and actively interested in them.

One technique to keep people talking is to echo their last phrase as a question and then add to it. If a person says 'So I decided to set up a new business', you can respond, 'Set up a new business? How have you found it?'

Good networkers:

- actively listen to what you say
- allow you to finish your response without interrupting
- make eye contact
- somehow make you feel special and interesting
- are helpful—provide referrals or give you information
- follow up when they say they will
- not only remember who you are the next time you meet, but also remember something about your previous conversation.

## Become a connector and referrer

Get people talking about why they are there and then play the host and introduce them to someone who may be useful to them.

As your list of contacts grows, you can also start making referrals. If you have a referral for someone, follow up after the meeting instead of waiting for the next meeting to give it to them.

> ## Blue Gum
> ### RESTAURANT
>
> Tania James was talking to an acquaintance, Janet, who had just moved into a new apartment. Janet was telling Tania how wonderful it was in the long summer evenings to sit out on the balcony and enjoy the view. She plans to make a balcony garden to give privacy from the neighbours and attract the birds.
>
> 'You must meet John Pettit,' said Tania. 'He has a balcony design service. He could help you choose the right plants for your area. I could introduce you, if you like.'

## Learn to move on

You can sometimes get stuck talking to someone and don't know how to escape. Although networking is about quality conversations rather than chalking up how many conversations you have, we've all had the experience of being stuck with people. When you're ready to move on, just excuse yourself with a remark like 'Excuse me, it was nice to meet you' or 'I enjoyed talking to you'.

If you feel you need to make an excuse, say you want to get some food or another drink, or talk to your friend who's just arrived. Remember you're at a networking function and the person you're talking to will probably be just as happy as you are to talk to other people.

If you're not good at extricating yourself from conversations, you could arrange with a friend beforehand to rescue you from conversations that have gone on too long. You could agree on a rescue signal, such as a wave, to let your friend know you need help.

Jane Amos had been talking to one person at a function for a while. She decided it was time to move on so she said: 'I'm here to network, so I'm going to keep circulating. It was lovely talking to you. Here's my business card. Have you got your business card with you? Thanks. I look forward to seeing you next time. Bye.'

# Follow up

Just as with friendships, your business networks will flourish through care and attention. Maintaining the relationships you make through networking will bring you the greatest professional results and the most personal satisfaction. As a general guide, spend about 50 per cent of your time following up with existing contacts and 50 per cent of your time on new contacts. Some of the new contacts will fizzle out, but it's usually impossible to tell at a first meeting who will become a useful contact or who will turn into a customer or client.

### Take action immediately

Sort your business cards as soon as you get back to your office or first thing the next day, or you'll soon forget the details of your conversations. Follow up with the new people you met within a week so you're still fresh in their minds. If, after a few networking meetings, you find that you get along particularly well with someone and your business relationship develops, then suggest meeting up again.

John Pettit met Molly, a fellow landscape gardener, at a networking event and discovered she was an expert in bromeliads and cacti. He rang her the next day.

John: 'I'd like to know more about what you do, as I'm interested in introducing a range of bromeliads into my shops. What say we meet for coffee?'

Molly: 'I'd love to, but I'm too busy at the moment preparing for the trade show next month.'

John: 'I'm going to be there too, so let's make a point of catching up for a coffee or a drink.'

## Use your database to keep in touch

If you have an electronic database, use the 'bring-up' system to follow up with everyone every three months, if not earlier—by phone, email or post. You don't have to have a reason for calling; you can just ring to keep in touch and see how they're going. By doing so you'll develop deeper relationships. If they're a prospective client or customer, you're also likely to be at the top of their minds if they need your product or service.

## Send thank-you notes

Many small businesses regularly send thank-you cards to suppliers, clients and customers. At their internal meetings, they'll think about who has helped them that week or that month and send them a card.

It's interesting when you make this a regular discipline to discover how many people do help you and how easy it is to take this help for granted. Saying 'thank you' doesn't take long, but makes a big difference to how your clients and customers remember you.

Send information of interest

One of the easiest ways of making contact with people after an event is to send them information that might interest them, such as an invitation to another networking group or an article you think they'd enjoy reading. Some people collect articles from magazines or the Internet so they can quickly sort through their resources to find a relevant article to send. Once you've sent the information, follow up a week later to find out whether it was useful.

Promote your products or services

When you follow up for the second or third time, you can start to talk about your products or services. You might suggest that you email, post or fax them some information for their own interest or in case they know of anyone else who may be interested in your business.

**Jane Amos**
NATURAL THERAPIST

Jane Amos often follows up with people she meets at networking functions with an offer of a discount for an introductory session for themselves or a family member. She either emails or posts this offer with a brochure about her business.

### Ask people whether they want your e-newsletter

E-newsletters are a great way of keeping in regular communication with people, but resist the temptation to sign up everyone you meet at networking events to your e-newsletter. You may not be breaking the law, but it is unprofessional and bad business practice to sign up people without asking their permission.

There are now so many e-newsletters in circulation that your e-newsletter needs to be distinctive or people will delete it without reading it. The most successful e-newsletters primarily provide content of interest to their readers. Over time, by providing a consistently interesting e-newsletter, you establish your credibility and develop a sense of community with your readers.

You can use your e-newsletters to promote your business, but in a low-key manner. For instance, I promote my courses in my e-newsletter, but it's never the first item.

## Online networking

Your website is also an integral part of all your marketing, as often people you meet at functions will visit your website to find out more about you. Your website needs to be in keeping with your brand, well written and regularly updated.

Some people create valuable networks online by participating in chat rooms and blogs. A blog is a web page made up of usually short, frequently updated posts that are arranged chronologically—like a 'what's new' page or a journal. The content and purposes of blogs varies greatly, from providing links and commentary about other websites, to news about a company/

person/idea, diaries, photos, poetry, mini-essays, project updates and even fiction.

Many people prefer emails to phone calls. You don't have to worry about whether or not the person is available at the time, and people can read them at their leisure. But your emails need to be personal, timely and of value.

If you want to send some information of interest to several people in your email address book, you can send the email to yourself and blind copy (Bcc) all the recipients. However, this email is no longer as personal. If you have the facility to set up personalised group emails, this is more effective than blind copying the entire group.

## Measure your networking

Do a return-on-investment (ROI) analysis of your networking over a period of time, such as a year. Your costs will include membership fees, cost of each meeting, parking and your time. Cost your time from the moment you leave your office to the moment you get back. Add up all the costs and you'll find that networking is probably more expensive than you realised. So, unless you're just networking to have fun, you definitely want a return on your investment.

To see what return you're getting, analyse your sales or invoices for the previous year. What business did you gain from networking and what was the dollar value of that networking for your business?

The intangible benefits—such as meeting with other people in your industry to keep up with the latest trends—are harder to measure, but write down your professional development and personal gains.

Then ask yourself if your networking is bringing you the rewards you want. If not, do you need to put your emphasis somewhere else? Alternatively, do you need to work more assiduously at networking so it brings you more profitable results?

### Delite Landscape DESIGN

John Pettit met a developer at a networking function who became a major client, commissioning Delite Landscape Design to do all the landscaping in a major new suburban development. The developer also allowed John to put his brochures in all the new apartments with balconies. John received several enquiries from these brochures, which led to further work.

Through attending industry educational evenings, John feels he's more in tune with the growing interest in sculptural gardens, rather than pretty cottage gardens, in inner-city living.

### Blue Gum RESTAURANT

Tania James and Bill Johnson both get a lot of personal satisfaction from their networking. Meeting other small businesspeople gives them a chance to view their own business with a clearer perspective. While this does not have a dollar value, Tania and Bill feel it's worthwhile for their business.

They have started to keep a list of people they meet at networking events who then come to their restaurant. To date, they estimate that about 3 per cent of the people they meet at events have come to their restaurant at least once.

>
> **Jane Amos**
> NATURAL THERAPIST
>
> Jane Amos attracts most of her business through networking and word of mouth. She keeps a simple spreadsheet listing the events she's attended, who she met for the first time, and who then booked a treatment session for themselves or a family member.
>
> At the end of the year she plans to refine her networking according to which events she enjoys most and which are most profitable for her business.

# Networking tips

In summary:

- attend as many of an organisation's events as you can
- join the organising committee
- put yourself in new networking situations regularly
- arrive early
- introduce yourself to speakers or panellists
- participate in sessions
- talk to people you don't know
- introduce people to each other
- follow up within a week
- keep in touch with contacts every three months
- carry business cards
- be a good listener.

# 5 Telemarketing

Telemarketing is fast, efficient and less expensive than many other marketing methods. You find out who the decision-makers are and receive immediate feedback. This allows you to screen out disinterested and unlikely prospects and concentrate on positive leads.

Over time, if you stay in regular contact with these leads, they move from cold to warm prospects and your phone calls become more personal and easier to make. You've now developed a relationship, which is the basis of most successful ongoing marketing.

Many companies will always be mildly dissatisfied with their current supplier, so if you ring and offer something better or different, they will probably be receptive. Alternatively, you may be lucky and they may have just identified a need when they receive your phone call.

Some businesses integrate telemarketing with their other marketing methods. For example, you can use telemarketing as a follow-up to a direct mail or email campaign. Many people find a follow-up phone call easier to make than a totally cold call. But even if you write a letter first, there is no guarantee that it will reach the right person so your phone call is still often a cold call.

You can also use telemarketing to get permission to send your prospects information via fax or email. When I started telemarketing, many people agreed to receive my e-newsletter. I think this may be harder now there are so many e-newsletters, but there's no harm in asking.

# Reasons why people fail at telemarketing

Many small business owners have an aversion to telemarketing, partly because telemarketing has such a bad reputation. While I was writing this chapter I paid particular attention to all the telemarketing calls I receive and was amazed at the poor quality of most of them. The telemarketers usually asked to speak to the 'business owner' and then delivered a pre-prepared spiel. They sounded unprofessional and they hassled me when I said I wasn't interested.

No self-respecting small business wants to sound like that. But you needn't. You can telemarket with integrity and sound professional.

Even once small business owners decide to telemarket, many still fail to achieve results because they make one or more of the following common mistakes.

## They have a fear of failure and rejection

When you look behind the excuses most people give for not telemarketing, the real reason is often fear—fear of failure and fear of rejection. These fears are real—you will often be rejected, and some people will be hostile or even openly rude to you. One way of identifying and facing your fears is to write them down and then look at them objectively. Remind yourself as you face those fears that the rejections aren't personal—the person on the other end of the phone has never met you.

### They give up too soon

Some people overcome their initial resistance to telemarketing, but then give up too soon. They underestimate how many calls it takes to make one sale or gain a new client. James Stapleton in *Developing a CPA Practice* (1997, pp. 137–50) recommends making at least a thousand calls before trying to gauge the initial success of your program.

James Stapleton says that at the time of writing his book, his accountancy firm wasn't listed in the top 25 companies in the area. Seven years after the firm began telemarketing, it was listed in Bowman's Top Ten Fastest-Growing Accounting Firms in the United States and was the largest independently owned company in its geographical area.

Seven other accounting firms started telemarketing programs at the same time and all seven eventually dropped them. Four ceased telemarketing after less than a month. Of the remaining three, two lasted less than six months, and the third folded its telemarketing program after a year. James Stapleton's firm had no success for the first two months either, yet persevered.

### They have a stop/start approach

Too many people use a stop/start approach to telemarketing. They telemarket when work dries up, then stop doing it when work picks up. The problem with this approach is there will usually be a delay between the time you start telemarketing and when you get new business.

To get the best results out of your telemarketing, you need to be continually ringing new contacts and at the same time ringing existing prospects so you're gently nudging them along. Many marketers follow a 90-day cycle and contact all their prospects regularly every three months.

At some point you need to decide when it's no longer productive to keep ringing someone and when to put that time and energy into developing new contacts instead. This decision needs to be based on the data you develop from monitoring and measuring your results, and on listening to your intuition.

In *Telesales* (2003, pp. 154–5), Stephan Schiffman says he was called in to help a Fortune 500 company improve the efficiency of its telesales force. When he analysed the numbers, he found that virtually no sales were closed on the fifth or subsequent calls, yet telemarketers kept on calling. By skipping the fifth call and making new calls instead, sales jumped 28 per cent in a month. On the other hand, I know of a company that persisted in ringing one prospect after most people would have stopped and on the ninth call gained a lucrative client.

## They fail to listen

In my opinion, the greatest mistake telemarketers make is failing to listen. The average telemarketer has a script and doesn't deviate from it. Listen to the telemarketing calls you receive and you'll see how true this is. While I think you need to develop a script and practise it, don't stick to it slavishly. Instead, aim to get the prospect talking and then listen so you can learn about their business and how you can help them. Successful telemarketing needs to be a dialogue.

## Getting started—what do you want to achieve?

As with any marketing, before you start you need to be clear about what you want to achieve, who your target market is, and what you have to offer that will be of interest and benefit to your prospects.

Your type of business will influence the approach you take. Some commodity businesses, such as companies that sell CDs, reasonably inexpensive software or telecommunication services, may want to make a sale over the phone. Other businesses with more complex products or services won't expect to make a direct sale with an initial phone call. The purchasing decision will take longer, so they'll take more of a 'softly, softly' approach.

Based on the knowledge that it may often take at least five or six phone calls to turn a prospect into a customer or client, you need to be clear what the aim of your first call is. It may be to get permission to ring again, send information, sign prospects up for your e-newsletter, or make an appointment.

Once you know what you want from the phone call, don't be afraid to ask for it. Many inexperienced telemarketers start conversations well, but are vague at the end. James Stapleton (1997) says that when he started asking people directly for appointments, his success rate soared.

If you're going to ask someone for an appointment, think about the words you use. If you think your prospects will be put off by words like 'appointment' or 'meeting' as they sound too formal, instead suggest that you 'come and see them'.

Making phone calls will get easier with time and your telephone techniques will improve, but there will always be an unpredictable element. You'll have days where nothing flows, yet on other days you'll strike a dream run and get several appointments in a row.

Start listening more closely to the telemarketing calls you receive. See how instinctively you put up a barrier when you realise it's a telemarketing call and look at how the telemarketer handles your resistance. I think the worst thing they can say is: 'How are you?': I immediately know it's a telemarketer as none of my clients or colleagues start a phone call that way.

Often, thinking about making calls is much worse than making them. When you're talking to people, not fictitious bogeys, your fears will recede. One piece of advice I received when starting out is to stand when making calls and smile as you talk. Your breathing is less constrained when you stand and your body is more relaxed. Try it and see whether it makes a difference for you.

## The research approach

Some businesses take a 'research' approach to telemarketing. For example, you may decide you want to enter a new market or expand your presence in that market, but you don't know enough about the need for your product or service to pitch appropriately. The best way to find out is to ask companies in your target market what they are currently doing, how effective it is and where the gaps are.

Draw up a questionnaire, then ring key players in the industry and interview them. Many people will give you information if your questionnaire is short and if you promise to give them the results of the survey.

Once you've collated and analysed the survey, you can ring back with the results. At this stage, based on what you've learnt about their industry, you can start talking constructively about doing business with your prospects.

## Blue Gum RESTAURANT

Blue Gum Restaurant decided that it wanted to market its function room to corporate clients for team-building dinners and other events, such as social dinners after board meetings.

Tania James and Bill Johnson share the restaurant's telemarketing. The aim of their first call was to get permission to email or post information about the restaurant, its function room and sample menus.

Before Blue Gum started telemarketing, Tania and Bill did a random survey of corporate clients—including current and past clients and unknown prospects—to identify what the need was for restaurant function rooms. This research confirmed what they suspected: while budgets were definitely tighter than previously, many departments still held team-building dinners after a day's training, board members still met for social dinners after a board meeting, and some managers took their teams out for a Christmas dinner.

## Delite Landscape DESIGN

Delite Landscape Design's target markets are property owners and renters, but John Pettit decided they would be too difficult to reach. Instead he's decided to target real estate agents and developers to encourage them to promote Delite's balcony services to their clients. He also wants to let them know about his rent-a-balcony garden service, which could appeal to people selling apartments.

His aim when telemarketing to real estate agents and developers is to make appointments so he can show them Delite's portfolio and give them some marketing material to pass on to their clients.

John gets his staff to do most of the telemarketing, but still makes a few calls himself each week.

Jane Amos wants to build greater awareness of her services in her community. Her target groups are working mothers, women going though menopause and sportspeople.

As these groups are very diverse, Jane relies a lot on referrals, so she's telemarketing to doctors, sports physiotherapists, play groups, kindergarten and play centres, schools and health food stores. She hopes these people will put her marketing material in their foyers or on their counters and promote her services by word of mouth.

# The list—your target market

Before you pick up the phone, you need to draw up a list of likely prospects from your target market. There is no one 'right way' of making a list. You can compile a list from the phonebook, but the problem with such a list is that you often won't know anything about the company and may waste time either researching endlessly or ringing people who have no interest in your business.

You can purchase lists from global companies like D&B (www.dnb.com) or Kompass (www.kompass.com). These lists have the advantage that they give you detailed information about the companies and key people within them. If you're planning to make telemarketing a regular part of your marketing strategy, buying a list before you start is a good investment.

Alternatively, you can make your own list. Your own list will be the most valuable, but compiling a list is time-consuming and if you have a reluctance to pick up the phone, you could be tempted to use this preparation time as an excuse to procrastinate.

### Delite Landscape DESIGN

John Pettit drew up a list of real estate agents from local real estate magazines, which are distributed free every week in suburban areas. He found out the names of major developers currently constructing new apartment buildings by driving around suburban areas near his stores and writing down the developers' names and contact details. He then looked them up on the Internet to find out more about them.

### Blue Gum RESTAURANT

Blue Gum Restaurant bought a database of corporate companies. Tania James and Bill Johnson share the telemarketing and they target medium-to-large organisations that are likely to have a human resources department.

>
> **Jane Amos**
> NATURAL THERAPIST
>
> Jane Amos drew up a list of doctors, sports physiotherapists, health food stores, preschool organisations and schools from her local phonebook.

Opinion varies about how much research to do before you start ringing people. While it's obviously an advantage if you know something about the company, too much research may inhibit your listening skills as you feel you already know the answers.

## Develop your database and recording systems

You need to develop database and recording systems before you start. One of the most successful telemarketers I know uses an entirely paper-based system, but most businesses these days prefer electronic records for their database.

You will probably work off a hard-copy list for initial phone calls, but as soon as a prospect warrants a follow-up call, add them to your database. You can use Microsoft Access or purchase a contact management software package, such as ACT! Apart from improved security—provided you back up your data regularly—a computer program has the added advantage that other people in your business can use your records.

Develop a 'bring-up' system for your follow-ups. Use the calendar in your software program or develop a paper system that works for you. Then use your system rather than ignoring it.

Whether you're using a paper or computer system, it's important to keep full records, such as the date of the call and a brief summary of the conversation (see Figure 5.1). This helps you make more meaningful follow-up conversations, especially if you include incidental personal details, such as the fact that the person is going on holiday or is very busy at the moment meeting an urgent deadline.

This sort of detail gives you an 'in' when you next ring and makes the phone call more personal. You may think at the time that you'll remember, but three months later you won't. It also means that if someone else makes the follow-up call, they have some knowledge and feel for the person they're ringing.

## Time management

Once you've set up your database and recording systems, it's time to think about slotting your telemarketing program into your busy schedule. Employing telemarketers has the advantage that your telemarketing will be done regularly. The advantage of doing your own telemarketing is that you believe in the value of your products or services and your sincerity and passion will come through in your phone calls.

If you and your staff are telemarketing, decide whether to make a certain number of calls each day or week, or dedicate set periods of time for your calls. I have tried both approaches and find having a set time each week works best for me. I do it this way because I have to psyche myself into ringing people and would rather go through that mental effort for a reasonable period of time once a week than do it daily. I do, however, make a few high-priority follow-up calls on a regular basis.

## Figure 5.1 Contact sheet

Telemarketer: _____

Company name: _____

Company address:

_____

_____

Company details:

_____

_____

Phone: _____   Fax: _____   Email: _____

Contact names:

| Name and position: | Phone: | Email: | Mobile: |
|---|---|---|---|
| _____ | _____ | _____ | _____ |
| _____ | _____ | _____ | _____ |
| _____ | _____ | _____ | _____ |

Date:

**Comments:**

_____

_____

_____

_____

_____

It's easy to procrastinate before telemarketing. Avoidance behaviours include reading emails, clearing your desk, filing papers, ringing friends or making another cup of tea or coffee. Keeping records of all the calls will help you monitor your behaviour so you become more efficient. Another way of avoiding procrastination is to thoroughly prepare the day before so you get straight into making phone calls the next day.

You'll find some days and times are more successful than others. There are different opinions about what time of day is best to call. Some say 'don't ring after 4 p.m.' and others find that prospects are more relaxed and open to calls at the end of the working day. Some people never ring on a Friday, while others devote Friday to telemarketing. Some telemarketers start early, say 7 a.m., to avoid the gatekeepers; others start at 8.30 a.m. when there's someone on the main switchboard.

## Making the calls

Once you've done your preparation, you're ready to start making the actual calls. It's also a good idea to set up your measurement systems before you start, so you're collecting meaningful data as you go.

Whenever possible, find out the name of the person you want to speak to and use their name in your opening statement. There's nothing more off-putting than 'Can I please speak to the business owner?' The prospect knows immediately it's a telemarketing call and their defences go up.

If you've bought a list, it may give you that information or, if you're ringing a reasonably sized organisation and know the job title of the person you want to speak to, ask the receptionist for the person's name and how to pronounce it correctly.

The best way to open any conversation is to greet the person by name. Opinions vary on whether to greet people by their first name (Jade), full name (Jade Smith) or with a title (Ms Smith). The choice you make depends on your personal preference and your knowledge of your target market.

## Gatekeepers

Many telemarketers make the mistake of treating gatekeepers (receptionists, secretaries and personal assistants) as unimportant 'bit' players. While you are going to have more immediate success if you have direct access to the decision-maker, often the only way to reach the decision-maker is through the gatekeeper, so treat them with respect. Address them by name, ask their advice and enlist their support. It's common courtesy and a good investment.

## The script

You need to have a well-prepared script that says precisely and succinctly what you want to say, yet still gives you room to engage the prospect in conversation. You have about 30 seconds at the most to grab your prospect's attention. Most people are immediately defensive when they receive telemarketing calls so you have to break through that reserve. You don't have the advantages that you do in face-to-face presentations of eye contact or props like sales brochures.

Many telemarketers read their script word-for-word and bulldoze their way through it until they've finished, without giving the prospect a chance to say a word. When they finally get to the end, the prospect says 'yes' or 'no' (mainly 'no') and that's the end of the conversation. That kind of call may strike it lucky, but it's generally a waste of a call. A good script sounds conversational, gets straight to the point and then gives the prospect an opportunity to talk.

Before you write your script, clarify in your mind what you have to offer that distinguishes you from other businesses and what will appeal to your prospects. If you're having difficulty articulating this, try writing down the reasons why people buy from you, or ring a few satisfied clients and customers and ask them why they use your products and services.

Once you've written your script, internalise it by learning it off by heart. Practise it by saying it out loud, speaking in front of a mirror, or talking into a tape recorder and playing it back to yourself.

## Structure of a telemarketing conversation

A telemarketing conversation has its own unique structure—and it's not the monologue you receive from far too many telemarketers.

### ATTENTION STATEMENT

The best way to get someone's attention is simply to address them by their name: 'Hi Joseph,' or 'Good morning Mr Smith.'

---

Delite Landscape DESIGN

John Pettit: 'Good afternoon. This is John Pettit from Delite Landscape Design.'

---

Blue Gum RESTAURANT

Tania James: 'Hi, I'm Tania James from Blue Gum Restaurant in Blues Point.'

>
>
> Jane Amos: 'Hi, I'm Jane Amos. I'm a natural therapist.'

### GIVE THE REASON FOR YOUR CALL

The next step is to give the reason for your call. This will usually be to explain how your product or service can benefit the prospect. It sounds simple, but the challenge here is to establish your credibility and gain their interest in a short space of time.

You can set yourself up as an expert by using phrases like 'we specialise in . . .', 'our reputation is . . .', 'we are known for . . .'. You could also drop in the names of clients or customers in their

> **Delite Landscape DESIGN**
>
> John Pettit to real estate agents: 'I'm calling to tell you about our rent-a-balcony garden service. When your clients put their apartments on the market, they can increase the value of their properties by transforming their balconies into private, attractive havens with our pots and planters.'

> **Blue Gum RESTAURANT**
>
> Tania James to corporate clients: 'The reason I'm calling is to let you know about our restaurant's function room, which is available for corporate dinners. Gillian Smith, from Hextons, recently used our function room for a team dinner, and she suggested that I give you a ring.'

industry, especially if they're success stories. This is a short-hand way of informing the prospect you understand their industry and it gives you credibility if they haven't heard of you. If someone has referred you, this is the time to mention it.

Jane Amos to doctor's receptionist: 'Hi Sandra, I'm ringing to let your practice know about my natural therapy services, which include sports massage, reiki, reflexology and Bowen therapy. I know you must get thousands of such calls, so why don't I pop in next Friday and give you a five-minute neck and shoulder massage?'

ASK OPEN-ENDED QUESTIONS

Once you have introduced yourself, try to get the prospect involved in a conversation by asking open-ended questions. Often their initial knee-jerk response is to get rid of you as fast as possible, but if you make a connection and get them talking, you'll increase their interest and involvement in the conversation.

The questions you ask must be relevant so, before you ring, make a list of questions that you would genuinely like to know about their business and practise asking one or two. Even if the prospect is not interested in your call, their answers may give you valuable information about their industry.

John Pettit to real estate agents: 'What difference do you think an attractive balcony garden makes to the sales price of an apartment?'

> **Blue Gum**
> **RESTAURANT**
>
> Tania James to corporate clients: 'Out of interest, what restaurants do you currently use for your social functions?'

>  **Jane Amos**
> **NATURAL THERAPIST**
>
> Jane Amos to doctor's receptionist: 'What sort of follow-up treatment does Dr White usually recommend for sports injuries?'

### ASK FOR WHAT YOU WANT

To close the conversation, ask for what you want. In most cases, unless you're aiming to make an immediate sale over the phone, this will usually be an appointment or their permission to email or post more information. Although meeting with someone may be your preferred option, getting permission to send information or call again can be a useful stepping stone in the marketing courtship.

Some telemarketers, when asking for an appointment, give people a choice of times, rather than asking them whether or not they want to meet. The rationale is that it's harder to say 'no' when presented with a choice than it is to say 'no' to a closed question.

> **Delite Landscape DESIGN**
>
> John Pettit: 'I can come and show you our design portfolio and give you some of our brochures. Does this Thursday suit you or would next Thursday be better?'

## Blue Gum RESTAURANT

Tania James: 'What's your email address so I can send you some information about our function room with some sample menus and prices?'

## Jane Amos NATURAL THERAPIST

Jane Amos: 'I'm going to be in your area next Wednesday. What would be the best time to pop in with some brochures?'

### THE 'YES' LADDER

Some telemarketers build a 'yes' ladder into their conversations. The theory is that prospects get into the rhythm of saying 'yes', so are more likely to say 'yes' when you ask for a meeting or make a proposition. This technique also weeds out unlikely prospects early on.

## Delite Landscape DESIGN

John Pettit uses the 'yes' ladder in follow-up calls:

- Did you receive my fax yesterday?
- Do you enjoy gardening?
- Are you familiar with plants that are drought resistant?
- Would you like me to send you some information about drought-resistant plants?

Jane Amos uses the 'yes' ladder when making an initial telemarketing call:

- Do you sometimes feel overwhelmed by everything you've got to do?
- Would you like more time out for yourself?
- Do you sometimes feel you need a relaxing massage to release all that tension in your muscles?
- Would you like me to make you an appointment for a massage next week?

## Not interested

Many people's immediate response will be 'not interested' because you're a cold call and you've disrupted them. Often, their lack of interest is genuine and you need to respect that, but sometimes 'never' means 'not now' or 'I'm not listening to you'. If you can create a dialogue to overcome this barrier, you can often turn this prospect around.

Write down all the excuses you expect to hear. They'll probably include:

- 'We already have another supplier.'
- 'We don't have the budget.'
- 'I'm too busy to think about it right now.'
- 'We don't need your product or service.'
- 'Where did you get my number?'

One way of turning the conversation around is to acknowledge their lack of interest and then state a benefit you've achieved with another customer or client. For example: 'Other businesses said the same thing until they found out how our (*product or service*) could benefit them. Using our (*product or service*), they found that (*state the benefit*).'

Alternatively, engage in a dialogue by asking them a question and opening a way to contact them later.

### Leaving messages

Some days as many as 75 per cent of people you call will be unavailable. Some telemarketers don't leave messages, but why waste a phone call? It's better to leave a message, especially if it is a follow-up phone call.

When you leave a message, leave your name, business name, reason for the call and your phone number. Voice messages are more effective if they're personal, so weave the prospect's name into your message.

Many people practise their scripts, but not their voice messages. Practise different messages on yourself before you use them. Listen to yourself honestly and ask yourself whether you'd return the call. If not, keep practising until you're satisfied.

When you leave your voice message, remember not to rush through it. Pause as you're speaking, say your name and phone number slowly and repeat the number so they don't have to replay the message to write it down.

## Measuring telemarketing success

Even if you have the right list, telemarketing is still a numbers game. Make yourself a simple call-tracking system to record all the calls you make on a daily or weekly basis (see Figure 5.2), then analyse the results in a monthly summary (see Figure 5.3). From this summary, you can work out how many calls it takes to make an appointment and generate new business. This analysis will also identify areas you need to improve, and any weak links. For example, are you getting appointments, but then failing to 'close the deal'?

Don't be too hard on yourself at first. You will improve with experience. James Stapleton (1997) says when he started telemarketing, he secured one meeting from every 300 calls. By the time he stopped, 40 000 calls later, his percentage was one meeting from every 30 calls.

**Figure 5.2  Call tracking sheet**

---

**Name of telemarketer:** _____  **Date:** _____

Fill in this sheet on a daily or weekly basis depending on how many calls you make. This form is divided into two sections so you will tick more than one box for each phone call. You may adapt the box to include more numbers if you are making a large number of calls.

**Section 1: Number of overall phone calls made per day or week**

**New contacts**

1–10   ❏ ❏ ❏ ❏ ❏ ❏ ❏ ❏ ❏ ❏
11–20  ❏ ❏ ❏ ❏ ❏ ❏ ❏ ❏ ❏ ❏

**Follow-up calls**

1–10   ❏ ❏ ❏ ❏ ❏ ❏ ❏ ❏ ❏ ❏
11–20  ❏ ❏ ❏ ❏ ❏ ❏ ❏ ❏ ❏ ❏

**Section 2: Response to calls**

**Unavailable**

1–10   ❏ ❏ ❏ ❏ ❏ ❏ ❏ ❏ ❏ ❏
11–20  ❏ ❏ ❏ ❏ ❏ ❏ ❏ ❏ ❏ ❏

**Not interested**

1–10  ☐ ☐ ☐ ☐ ☐ ☐ ☐ ☐ ☐ ☐

11–20 ☐ ☐ ☐ ☐ ☐ ☐ ☐ ☐ ☐ ☐

**Left message**

1–10  ☐ ☐ ☐ ☐ ☐ ☐ ☐ ☐ ☐ ☐

11–20 ☐ ☐ ☐ ☐ ☐ ☐ ☐ ☐ ☐ ☐

**Deliver/send info**

1–10  ☐ ☐ ☐ ☐ ☐ ☐ ☐ ☐ ☐ ☐

**Want e-newsletter**

1–10  ☐ ☐ ☐ ☐ ☐ ☐ ☐ ☐ ☐ ☐

**Appointments**

1–10  ☐ ☐ ☐ ☐ ☐ ☐ ☐ ☐ ☐ ☐

**Summary No.**

New calls          _____

Follow-up calls    _____

**Total calls**    _____

**Response to calls**

Unavailable        _____

Not interested     _____

Left message       _____

Delivered/sent info _____

Wanted e-newsletter _____

Appointments       _____

From this information, you can over time work out how many calls it takes you to make an appointment and gain new business. I also find it helpful to look at the value of new business I get through telemarketing (see Figure 5.4).

**Example: Call tracking sheet**

**Jane Amos**
NATURAL THERAPIST

Name of telemarketer: _Jane Amos_    Date: _5 October_

**Section 1: Number of overall phone calls made per day or week**

**New contacts**

| Range | 1 | 2 | 3 | 4 | 5 | 6 | 7 | 8 | 9 | 10 |
|---|---|---|---|---|---|---|---|---|---|---|
| 1–10 | ☑ | ☑ | ☑ | ☑ | ☑ | ☑ | ☑ | ☑ | ☑ | ☑ |
| 11–20 | ☑ | ☑ | ☑ | ☑ | ☑ | ☑ | ☑ | ☑ | ☐ | ☐ |

**Follow-up calls**

| Range | 1 | 2 | 3 | 4 | 5 | 6 | 7 | 8 | 9 | 10 |
|---|---|---|---|---|---|---|---|---|---|---|
| 1–10 | ☑ | ☑ | ☑ | ☑ | ☑ | ☑ | ☑ | ☑ | ☑ | ☑ |
| 11–20 | ☑ | ☑ | ☐ | ☐ | ☐ | ☐ | ☐ | ☐ | ☐ | ☐ |

**Section 2: Response to calls**

**Unavailable**

| Range | 1 | 2 | 3 | 4 | 5 | 6 | 7 | 8 | 9 | 10 |
|---|---|---|---|---|---|---|---|---|---|---|
| 1–10 | ☑ | ☑ | ☑ | ☑ | ☑ | ☑ | ☑ | ☑ | ☑ | ☑ |
| 11–20 | ☑ | ☑ | ☐ | ☐ | ☐ | ☐ | ☐ | ☐ | ☐ | ☐ |

**Not interested**

| Range | 1 | 2 | 3 | 4 | 5 | 6 | 7 | 8 | 9 | 10 |
|---|---|---|---|---|---|---|---|---|---|---|
| 1–10 | ☑ | ☑ | ☑ | ☑ | ☑ | ☑ | ☑ | ☑ | ☐ | ☐ |
| 11–20 | ☐ | ☐ | ☐ | ☐ | ☐ | ☐ | ☐ | ☐ | ☐ | ☐ |

**Left message**

| Range | 1 | 2 | 3 | 4 | 5 | 6 | 7 | 8 | 9 | 10 |
|---|---|---|---|---|---|---|---|---|---|---|
| 1–10 | ☑ | ☑ | ☑ | ☑ | ☑ | ☑ | ☐ | ☐ | ☐ | ☐ |
| 11–20 | ☐ | ☐ | ☐ | ☐ | ☐ | ☐ | ☐ | ☐ | ☐ | ☐ |

**Deliver/send info**

| Range | 1 | 2 | 3 | 4 | 5 | 6 | 7 | 8 | 9 | 10 |
|---|---|---|---|---|---|---|---|---|---|---|
| 1–10 | ☑ | ☑ | ☑ | ☑ | ☐ | ☐ | ☐ | ☐ | ☐ | ☐ |

**Want e-newsletter**

| Range | 1 | 2 | 3 | 4 | 5 | 6 | 7 | 8 | 9 | 10 |
|---|---|---|---|---|---|---|---|---|---|---|
| 1–10 | ☑ | ☑ | ☑ | ☑ | ☐ | ☐ | ☐ | ☐ | ☐ | ☐ |

**Appointments**

| Range | 1 | 2 | 3 | 4 | 5 | 6 | 7 | 8 | 9 | 10 |
|---|---|---|---|---|---|---|---|---|---|---|
| 1–10 | ☑ | ☑ | ☐ | ☐ | ☐ | ☐ | ☐ | ☐ | ☐ | ☐ |

| Summary | No. |
|---|---|
| New calls | 18 |
| Follow-up calls | 12 |
| **Total calls** | 30 |
| **Response to calls** | |
| Unavailable | 12 |
| Not interested | 8 |
| Left message | 6 |
| Delivered/sent info | 4 |
| Wanted e-newsletter | 4 |
| Appointments | 2 |

**Figure 5.3  Overall monthly summary**

| Monthly summary sheet | No. |
|---|---|
| New calls | _____ |
| Follow-up calls | _____ |
| **Total calls** | _____ |
| **Response to calls** | |
| Unavailable | _____ |
| Not interested | _____ |
| Left message | _____ |
| Delivered/sent info | _____ |
| Wanted e-newsletter | _____ |
| Appointments | _____ |

| Monthly summary sheet | No. |
|---|---|
| New calls | 318 |
| Follow-up calls | 113 |
| **Total calls** | 431 |
| **Response to calls** | |
| Unavailable | 180 |
| Not interested | 83 |
| Left message | 45 |
| Delivered/sent info | 43 |
| Wanted e-newsletter | 82 |
| Appointments | 43 |

**Jane Amos**
NATURAL THERAPIST

Jane Amos was initially not pleased with the results of her telemarketing because when she visited prospects a week after posting them her brochures she found that very few places were displaying them prominently. She checked again a few weeks later and found that the display rate was much better after her personal visit. She now realises that, as her target market is local, she needs to deliver the brochures in person instead of posting them.

## Figure 5.4
### New business acquired through telemarketing

| Name of client/customer | Type of product/service | Length of time it took to acquire the client | $ value of new business |
|---|---|---|---|
| | | | |
| | | | |
| | | | |

### Example: New business acquired through telemarketing

| **Jane Amos** NATURAL THERAPIST | | | |
|---|---|---|---|
| Name of client/customer | Type of product/service | Length of time it took to acquire the client | $ value of new business |
| Dr John Smith | Sports massage for patients | 2 months | $1400 to date |
| | | | |
| | | | |

# 6 Public speaking

Public speaking is great promotion as your name appears in front of a wide range of people, both in the promotion for the event and at the actual event. If you're not very experienced at giving speeches, getting started may seem daunting. You may want to take some classes or get some coaching before you start, but remember you'll never feel completely ready and you'll learn more from speaking to an audience than practising. Many people find that once they've overcome their nerves, they enjoy the thrill of public speaking.

It's not difficult to find speaking opportunities once you start looking. Groups are always looking for interesting speakers and you can talk to a wide range of professional, business, academic and industry groups at conferences, meetings and seminars. Often you won't be paid for public speaking, but if you find you enjoy giving speeches you can make public speaking part of your business, not just a marketing tool, and look for paid speaking assignments.

# Is public speaking for you?

Many people are afraid of public speaking and, as Jerry Seinfeld said in a monologue in episode 61 of *Seinfeld*: 'According to most studies, people's number one fear is public speaking. Number two is death. Death is number two. Does that seem right? That means to the average person if you have to go to a funeral, you're better off in the casket than doing the eulogy.'

If that sums up your attitude to public speaking, then it may not be for you.

Another concern is that you're giving away a lot of intellectual property for nothing. This can be a real problem if you're asked to give free workshops, but a speech will often whet people's appetites for more information. After listening to your speech, they may want to book you as a speaker for another event or find out more about your business.

Marketing yourself as a speaker and preparing for speeches won't cost you much money, but it is time-consuming, especially when you are just starting out. Although you may develop generic topics, you will still need to tailor each speech so it is suitable for a particular audience or in case people in the audience have heard you talk before. You need to decide whether the time you spend preparing and delivering speeches is worth the return to your business.

# Plan your public speaking approach

One of the main advantages of public speaking is that it helps build your reputation as an expert in your field and raises your profile in your industry or community. You may get business directly from a speech, but more often your speech will be the beginning of a relationship with the people in the audience, so you need to find ways of keeping in touch with them. Many speakers put their brochures and business cards on everybody's seats. Some also include a voucher offering a discount on their product or service. For example, a sweet shop may offer a free box of chocolates with a $10 or more purchase in the next month.

If you have products to sell, such as CDs, tapes, books or gift vouchers, you can often arrange for a friend or associate to sell these before and after your speech.

John Pettit uses public speaking to:

- maintain a high profile in the community
- encourage people to visit his shops
- raise interest in the products and services he offers
- encourage people to use his balcony design services.

Tania James and Bill Johnson went to Toastmasters together to learn public speaking skills. They use public speaking to:

- maintain their profile in the community
- tell people what is special about their restaurant
- establish themselves as leaders in the restaurant trade
- help other people who want to enter the restaurant trade
- gain more customers.

**Jane Amos**
NATURAL THERAPIST

Jane Amos is relatively new to public speaking so she is willing to speak at any event to increase her confidence. She wants to use public speaking to:

- educate people about healthy living
- explain the therapies she uses
- establish herself as an expert in her field
- gain more clients.

## Identify speaking opportunities

Think about what target markets you want to reach with your public speaking and look for speaking engagements that will reach those audiences. Speaking to audiences outside your target market may be good experience, but may not grow your business unless people recommend your products and services.

The easiest way to find out what events your clients or customers attend is to ask them. They will often tell you about organisations that you didn't even know existed. If your target market is business, you could contact your local chamber of commerce, SWAP group, or local associations of retired and semi-retired professionals and businesspeople such as Rotary, Lions or Probus clubs.

Once you've drawn up a list of potential speaking opportunities, contact the organisation and find out who's responsible for arranging speakers. You need to develop an ongoing relationship with event organisers, so create a database and system for recording notes about your conversations with each person and organisation you contact.

## Delite Landscape DESIGN

- *Probus clubs*—John Pettit talks to Probus groups once a year in all three cities he has stores in.
- *Gardening groups*—John and staff members frequently talk at local gardening groups on specific topics, such as how to prune roses, and inner-city gardening.
- *Developers and real estate agents*—John talks at urban development and real estate conferences.

## Blue Gum RESTAURANT

- *Food and wine groups*—Bill Johnson and Tania James talk at food and wine groups about food trends.
- *Lions, Rotary groups and local chambers of commerce*—Bill and Tania talk to business groups about the challenges and joys of setting up and running a restaurant.
- *Pre-school and school committees*—Bill and Tania talk to pre-school and school committees on a wide range of topics including menus for special occasions and running a small family business.

## Jane Amos NATURAL THERAPIST

- *Health and well-being conferences*—Jane Amos talks at conferences on the value natural therapies have for overall well-being.
- *Natural therapy professional association meetings*—Jane talks at meetings about Bowen therapy.

- *Pre-school and school committee meetings*—Jane talks to pre-school and committee meetings about life and work balance.
- *Women's business groups*—Jane talks to women's groups about relaxation techniques they can use in their busy lives.
- *Sports clubs*—Jane talks to sports groups about how to prepare their bodies for peak performance.

## Write a speaking proposal

Many event organisers will want a speaking proposal to demonstrate what you have to offer the audience. Include an outline of your topic or topics, a brief bio in paragraph form (preferably with a photo), your public speaking experience and testimonials. Some speakers also send a CD or tape with excerpts from recent speeches.

### DEVELOP SPEAKING TOPICS

Audiences want to be entertained as well as educated. The most moving speeches are based on personal knowledge and experience. Choose a topic that you can speak about with conviction. If you're passionate about your topic, your enthusiasm will show in your speaking.

You need to develop topics *related* to your business, not *about* your business. This may sound obvious, but some speakers make the mistake of using a speech to directly promote their business. You are unlikely to be invited to speak for that organisation again. There are, of course, exceptions—for example, if you are asked to talk about why you started your business or how you grew your business to the next level.

Many public speakers choose a narrow range of topics and seek to gain a reputation as an expert in that field. Have a look at some professional speakers' websites (you can find speaker directories through the National Speakers Association—www.nsaspeakers.org). Topics on the National Speakers' website are categorised by interest areas, ranging from advertising and public relations through to magic, technology and retirement.

Once you've selected your topic or topics, see if they come under a general heading, such as 'Marketing' or 'Lifestyle'. That will help you market your speeches to the most appropriate organisations.

---

## Delite Landscape DESIGN

John Pettit categorises his speaking topics as 'lifestyle—gardening'. His topics include:

- do-it-yourself gardens—how to design your own garden
- seasonal tips—planting, pruning and maintenance tips for all seasons
- how to design and care for a balcony garden
- how to grow a bountiful vegetable garden in a small space
- planting for your conditions—drought-resistant plants for hot climates.

---

## Blue Gum RESTAURANT

Tania James and Bill Johnson categorise their speaking topics as 'small family business' and 'lifestyle'. They have developed the following speaking topics:

- how to run a successful restaurant business
- how to survive your family business
- healthy cooking for busy families.

Public speaking 111

Jane Amos categorises her speaking topics as 'health', 'self-esteem' and 'lifestyle'. She speaks about:

- the power of breathing
- me first—the benefits of looking after yourself
- sport and relaxation
- massage and menopause.

FLESH OUT YOUR SPEAKING TOPICS

Organisers will often want more information about your topic and may ask you to write a blurb for their website or promotional material. Write a few paragraphs for each topic that you could easily tailor for specific audiences.

### Me first—the benefits of looking after yourself

Before take-off in a plane, you're told that in an emergency you must put on your own oxygen mask before fitting one on your child. The same principle applies in life. As a working mum, you must put your own health and well-being first if you're going to cope with the competing demands of work, children and the home. It's commonsense, yet it's advice that's too often ignored.

Jane takes a practical, down-to-earth approach to this subject and talks about massage and breathing techniques that even the busiest woman can fit into her schedule. Her speech includes some fun hands-on exercises to get your energy flowing more freely. She'll give you relaxation tips you can use while standing at the supermarket check-out or when you're stuck in traffic.

After hearing Jane speak, you'll walk out feeling relaxed and energised and you'll also take with you some simple self-nurturing tips you can use in your everyday life.

WRITE A BRIEF PROFILE

You also need to write a brief profile about yourself to establish your credibility and for the organiser to use to promote the event. You may want to send two versions—a one-page profile for the organiser's information and a few paragraphs suitable for their promotional material.

John Pettit is a qualified landscape designer. He founded Delite Landscape Design 27 years ago. His business, which has branches in three cities, offers landscape gardening services. In recent years, John has specialised in inner-city gardening—courtyards, patios and balconies. He particularly enjoys creating vegetable and herb gardens in small spaces.

Tania James and Bill Johnson talk about the ups and downs of setting up a family restaurant business. They set up Blue Gum Restaurant together—and they're still talking to each other. Bill's background in accounting helps, while Tania is responsible for the day-to-day running of the restaurant.

**Jane Amos**
NATURAL THERAPIST

Jane Amos has worked in the healthcare field for more than 15 years. With a background as a nurse, Jane first became interested in natural therapies when she had her first child. She completed a degree in naturopathy by correspondence while bringing up her two children on her own and working part time. She knows from first-hand experience that when you try to be superwoman, something has to give—and it's often your health.

Taking the first public speaking steps

If you're new to public speaking, you need to learn some public speaking skills before attempting to get onto the speaking circuit. You could join Toastmasters (an international public speaking organisation with clubs in approximately 80 countries around the world), attend a public speaking workshop, or find an individual speaking coach.

To gain experience, you may choose speaking engagements with small groups or talk to groups in the outskirts of your region. Such speaking engagements will give you valuable confidence and experience. When you start out, finding the first speaking gig seems daunting, but someone will give you a lucky break and then you're on your way.

# Prepare your speech

When preparing a speech, the first step is to find out as much information as you can about the audience so you can tailor your speech to suit them. Then plan a structure for your speech so you have a logical theme running through it. Think of the structure from your audience's point of view, rather than what makes sense to you.

If you're giving the same speech several times to different groups, you can make it more lively by using different examples and stories. Some speakers collect magazine and newspaper clippings or keep a journal of stories or ideas.

## Common speech structures

Remember when planning your speech that less is more. There's only room for three or four main ideas, supported by evidence, case studies and anecdotes.

### LOGICAL SEQUENCE
You can start from the beginning or first step and move logically through to a conclusion or final point. For example, if you're talking about marketing, you could talk about clarifying your purpose, identifying your audience, determining your budget, choosing marketing tools and writing an action plan.

### PROBLEM AND SOLUTIONS
A useful structure, particularly for persuasive speeches, is to present a problem and then identify the solution. Using this structure, you can tell your audience what is wrong, explain why it is wrong, suggest how the situation could be corrected, and explain what they can do about it.

### CHRONOLOGICAL
With a chronological order you present your ideas according to the time they occurred—starting at either the beginning or end point. For example, you could look at the history of technology in personal communications, from the telephone through to emails and mobile messaging systems.

## Public speaking

### Q&As

You know what your audience is interested in from the questions you're frequently asked about your area of expertise. In your speech, pose these questions and then answer them. For example, 'The question I'm most frequently asked about running a restaurant is . . .'

### Past–present journey formula

In this speech, you tell your audience a three-part story: this is where I was, this is where I am, and this is how I got here. This structure is particularly useful for personal stories of achievement.

## Openings

The first and last 30 seconds of your speech make the most impact, so spend time perfecting them and making sure they're appropriate for your audience. Common mistakes are time-wasting remarks such as 'It's nice to be here', apologetic remarks like 'I haven't got much time', a story or joke that doesn't relate to the topic, or trite questions such as 'Have you ever stopped to think about . . . ?'

You can make a statement that grabs attention, relate a story, ask a question, tell a joke, or use a quote. Whatever method you use, you need to create a bond with your audience, arouse their interest and establish goodwill.

*Blue Gum*
RESTAURANT

Bill Johnson opened his speech to a Rotary group about setting up a restaurant like this:

> I'm often asked what made me set up a restaurant business in my forties when I already had a perfectly satisfying job. I'd love to say I had a burning desire to own a restaurant all my life, but it would be a lie.
>
> Owning and running a restaurant actually came about as a result of a chance comment by my wife. A small group of us who had all recently turned 40 were dining at a local restaurant. As we dined, we talked about what we wanted to do with the rest of our lives. Having more fun was top of everyone's agenda and my wife turned to me and said jokingly: 'We should open a restaurant. That'd be fun.'
>
> That chance remark turned our lives around. And we naively imagined it would be fun! Well, it has been fun, and still is, but it's also hard work. This evening I'm going to tell you about some of the challenges we encountered in our first year of business and how we dealt with them.

## Closing

A weak or apologetic finish can let down an otherwise good speech. It's like standing on the punchline of a joke. Your conclusion should inform the listener you're about to finish, summarise the main ideas, and leave the audience with something to think about or an idea to remember.

# Speech writing tips

Some people write their speech in full and then memorise the main ideas, some write a few key points or a PowerPoint presentation and then rehearse the speech, and others write their speeches entirely in their heads and never put pen to paper. When I first started giving speeches at Toastmasters, I used to write notes and use cards as prompts. As I became more confi-

John Pettit: 'So now you've learnt how to grow a bountiful garden in a small space, you can make yourself a home-grown salad, open a chilled bottle of wine and sit on your balcony and watch your tomatoes grow.'

dent, I moved to rehearsing speeches in my head or out loud without writing any notes at all. I still prefer 'writing' speeches that way.

## Tell stories that relate to your topic

People like listening to stories and anecdotes. A good story will stay in your audience's mind longer than any other part of your speech and they may even repeat your story to their friends. Your stories don't have to be long, but they do have to be relevant and relate to your theme.

### STORYTELLING TIPS

Tell your own stories, rather than other people's stories. Your own stories are always more powerful than borrowed tales. If you do want to use other people's stories, acknowledge them as such.

- Choose a short, simple story which relates to just one incident.
- Use concrete details rather than abstract ideas. The more specific you are, the more people will be able to visualise the situation ('At two o'clock on Saturday afternoon in a crowded supermarket...').
- Use dialogue to add pace to your story.

- Close quickly after the punchline. Avoid the temptation to add extra information or comment on your story.
- Use humour, but use it judiciously as you don't want to make a joke that no one laughs at.

John Pettit related this story in a speech to a Probus group:

Gardening can change your quality of life. One of my clients, Sally, had never had a garden until she moved into a townhouse with a small patio garden. She loved flowers but hated the thought of gardening. Her mother had a vegetable garden the size of a tennis court, and grew fruit and prize-winning daffodils, but Sally had always hated the gritty feel of dirt underneath her fingernails and watching worms die on the concrete path after it rained.

When she established her patio garden, Sally discovered she did, after all, inherit her mother's love of gardening. She also discovered the joy of pride: pride in eating lettuces from the garden, pride in being able to pick flowers for friends, and pride in watching the birds visit.

When Sally sold her townhouse, the garden was a huge selling point and her townhouse went for $15 000 more than a similar one had sold for in the previous month.

## Use statistics

Numbers and statistics can help you make a statement more meaningful; and statistics, like stories, are memorable—particularly if they are startling. For example, if you were talking about marathons, you could mention that it takes an army ant five-

and-a-half hours to walk a kilometre. Or, if you were talking about body image, you could mention that the most body piercings on a human is 462, of which 192 are on that person's head (statistics by Professor John Croucher, Macquarie University, Sydney).

### Use repetition for effect

You can repeat a word or phrase for emphasis or to make a point. An example is John Kennedy's famous sentence: 'And so, my fellow Americans: ask not what your country can do for you—ask what you can do for your country.'

Throughout history, three has been a significant number: some examples are three wishes; the three little pigs; faith, hope and charity; ready, aim, fire; red, amber, green; the good, the bad and the ugly; the past, present and future. You could think of three points you want to make or look at three aspects of the same topic.

Jane Amos: 'To have good health, you need to eat well, exercise and pamper yourself. Eating well will keep you healthy, exercising will keep your body trim and fit, and pampering yourself will give you that extra zest for life.'

### Be politically correct

As a public speaker, you don't want to intentionally offend anyone in your audience. If someone takes offence at something you say, it can undermine the value of your whole speech.

Many people take offence at swearing, racist jokes and sexist remarks, such as 'my wife spends all my money'. Many experienced speakers make these mistakes—don't be one of them.

### Polish and practise your speech

Polishing your speech is like editing written copy. Go through it and ask yourself 'Does it work?' or will people respond 'So what?' Be ruthless and delete any repetitions (unless used for emphasis), clichés and risky humour. When you're listening to yourself, listen for filler words like 'er' and 'um' and see if you've got a favourite word you overuse. Also, pay attention to your pace—many novice public speakers speak too fast and don't pause often enough.

Ideally, you should give a speech without referring to your notes. You need to be so familiar with your material that, although you may have prompt notes with you, you won't need them. If you're new to public speaking—or are developing a new speech—you may want to write your speech in full and record it. Say it out loud to yourself or practise in front of a mirror, and time how long your speech takes. Don't learn your speech word-for-word or it will lose spontaneity and come across as wooden. If you have friends or colleagues willing to listen to you, use them as your practice audience.

## Delivering your speech

Check out beforehand how formal the occasion is so you dress appropriately. As a general rule, you'll probably feel more comfortable if you veer on the side of too formal rather than informal and wear dark colours rather than pastels. Formal dress in dark colours makes you look more authoritative.

Arrive at the event venue early so you're comfortable with the environment and can check out the equipment. Don't rely on the room being the way you expect it to be or assume the technology will work. I've turned up to a venue with a PowerPoint presentation only to find that I was speaking in a long, narrow room unsuitable for PowerPoint. Another time I was promised an online connection for my PowerPoint presentation and didn't receive it. So turn up prepared to speak without any visual aids.

You will have sent through your profile to the organisation beforehand, but it may not have reached the person introducing you. If the person introducing you does not have an up-to-date bio, you can either give them a script to read (see Chapter 2 for a sample introduction) or tell them a few key points you'd like them to stress.

## Speaking, moving, eye contact and voice

We all have gestures we use without realising it. Try and eliminate all nervous and distracting mannerisms by watching yourself on a video or asking a friend or colleague for honest feedback.

Stand still when you start speaking so you look solid, confident and self-assured. You won't stand in the same position throughout your speech, but when you do move, move on a natural transition in your speech or to emphasise a point. Once you've stopped moving, reposition yourself.

It isn't possible to make an emotional connection with your audience without eye contact. No matter how big or small your audience, everyone wants to feel a sense of personal connection with you. In a small group, you'll be able to make contact with everyone, but in a large group that's not possible, so you need to make eye contact with a few individuals in each section of the room.

You will have timed your speech during your rehearsal, so make sure you stick to time when you're delivering it. Wear a watch or take a small clock with you to monitor your time. People start getting restless when a speaker goes on too long, no matter how good the speech is.

## Capitalise on your speech

You may be lucky and someone in the audience may be so impressed by your speech that they come up to you afterwards and buy your products and services then and there. But more often your speech is the beginning of a relationship, so you need to find ways of coming to the audience's attention again.

### Give another speech

Deliver another speech at a later date for the same organisation. Giving a good speech is not enough to guarantee a repeat invitation as there will always be several people vying for speaking slots. To be invited back you need to nurture your relationship with the event organiser. Drop out of touch for several months and you have to start marketing from scratch again.

### Give material to your audience

Many speakers put their promotional material on everyone's chairs so people can read about their business and know how to contact them after the event. You could also include an order form for your products or services.

You can also give everyone in the audience a hand-out of the key points of your speech or a copy of an article you've written. Make sure your name and contact details are prominently displayed on all your hand-outs.

### Follow up personally

Sometimes, the event organisers will give you the contact details of everyone who attended and you can ring or email them yourself. If you are going to contact people from the audience, you need to do it shortly after the event or you'll lose the moment.

### Ask people to subscribe to your e-newsletter

If you have an e-newsletter, you can ask people in the audience if they'd like to subscribe. One way of doing that is to give away a gift associated with your business, such as a book or free consultation. When people put their business cards into the container for the draw, you can ask them to add an 'e' if they'd like your e-newsletter. Sometimes the organisers like to keep these business cards, but will be prepared to give you a list of everyone who said 'yes' to your e-newsletter.

If you don't have a gift to give away, you can put a subscription form on each person's chair and ask them to fill it out and either leave it on their chair or hand it to you on their way out.

### Make a special offer

You can make a special offer to people in the audience, such as a discount for the following month. This offer needs to be worthwhile and time-limited to motivate people to take advantage of it.

### Sell products at the event

If you have products you can sell, most organisers will allow you to sell them before and after the event. Selling products yourself is a hassle, however, as you can't mingle with the audience, so try to get someone else to do the selling for you. Sometimes event organisers will arrange for everyone in the audience to get your product for an extra charge included in the booking fee.

To make the most of his speaking events, John Pettit:

- has a lucky business card draw with a pot plant as a prize and invites people to sign up to Delite's e-newsletter
- puts a flyer on each person's chair offering them a discount in his shop which is valid for the next two weeks
- stays in touch with the event organisers.

At their speaking events, Tania James and Bill Johnson:

- have a lucky business card draw for a meal for two and invite people to subscribe to their e-newsletter
- put a brochure on each chair about the restaurant and function room
- stay in touch with the event organisers.

**Jane Amos**
NATURAL THERAPIST

To make the most of her speaking events, Jane Amos:

- gives everyone a copy of her PowerPoint presentation with her contact details prominently displayed
- places a discount coupon which is valid for the next month on each person's chair
- stays in touch with the event organisers.

# Monitor and measure your results

You may have to give a number of speeches before you can judge whether or not they are effective for your business. Keep a record of your speeches and note what work comes out of each so you can make an objective assessment of their value. This record will also help you narrow your target market for speeches—some audiences may be much more profitable than others.

Sometimes, you may not receive any work directly from a speech, but you need to remember that everything you do has

*Blue Gum*
RESTAURANT

Tania James and Bill Johnson find they get a steady trickle of new customers as a result of their public speaking. They also know they have helped one or two people who were considering entering the restaurant business take the plunge. They believe every free promotional opportunity helps establish Blue Gum Restaurant as a quality restaurant that's in the market to stay.

John Pettit has built his e-newsletter database substantially from giving speeches. Every time he makes a promotional offer in his e-newsletter, sales increase at his garden stores. He now finds his e-newsletter a more successful sales tool than advertising.

John asks everyone who enquires about his balcony design service how they heard about Delite, and an increasing number are now saying they heard him give a speech or a friend heard him speak.

Although John has never measured the impact of maintaining a high profile in the community, he noticed that sales dropped slightly when he took an extended holiday earlier in the year.

At this stage, only a small percentage of Jane Amos's clients come from her speaking engagements. She finds that a few people in every audience take advantage of her discount coupon, but only one or two become regular clients. However, it's early days, so Jane is willing to give public speaking more time before deciding whether it's worth it for her business.

a cumulative effect and the more people hear about you, the more desirable your products and services become. You need to make a subjective evaluation of how effective speeches are in giving you a presence and profile in the community.

# 7 Running seminars

Seminars are a very successful way of promoting your business as they position you as an expert in your field and give you an occasion to play host to your clients, customers and prospects. Your customers and clients will appreciate that you're giving something back to them by sharing your knowledge, ideas and skills.

Seminars also allow you to demonstrate, rather than assert, your usefulness to prospects. Since most prospects will initially be sceptical about you and reluctant to expose their problems before they trust you, attending a seminar is a safe way of checking you out before committing themselves to buying from you.

In *Managing the Professional Services Firm,* David H. Maister (1993) goes as far as to say that seminars, if done well, top the list of effective marketing tools. He says that marketing is a seduction rather than an assault, and a seminar is concrete evidence of why prospects should get to know you better.

If you decide to run seminars, you need to decide how often you'll run them. Will you just do occasional seminars to inform clients or customers about industry news that affects them, such as new legislation, or will you run regular seminars on more general topics of interest?

If you run regular seminars, decide how often you can realistically manage them. I know of several companies that started running seminars with a great flourish and then fizzled out after a month or two once they realised how much they cost and how much work was involved.

The costs of running seminars are not insignificant, so draw up a budget before you start. Your costs will include room hire if you need to use a room outside your office, catering—even if it's just tea and coffee—name tags, worksheets and promotional flyers or brochures.

Running seminars is also a lot of work and you need to factor your time into your budget. To run successful seminars you must enjoy organising events—or be able to delegate the job—and have the fortitude to handle the things that will inevitably go wrong. Having run seminars myself and been a guest presenter at others, I know this to be true. My experiences include ordering some vegetarian sandwiches and not receiving any, the courier locking the workbooks in storage instead of delivering them for a weekend conference, and names spelt incorrectly. You'll ride out these mishaps and most participants won't even be aware that anything's amiss, but you have to keep smiling as if nothing's wrong.

If you decide running your own seminars is not for you, you can always make yourself available as a presenter for seminars run by other people. That way you get the benefit of the promotion from the event without having to organise it yourself.

# Should you charge for your seminars?

Many promotional seminars are free, but some businesses charge to either cover costs or make a profit. Whether you charge or not will depend on what you want to achieve and who you are inviting. If you're inviting special clients and customers, you may want to make your seminar free as a thank-you for their loyalty and custom.

The advantage of free seminars for your clients and customers is they will attend expecting to learn something of interest in a relaxed environment. They may also see it as a networking opportunity. They will not be expecting, nor should they receive, a sales pitch. Your guests are already your clients and customers, and the free seminar is a way of cementing the relationship. You can, of course, follow up afterwards and at this stage you can talk about your business and ask for referrals.

If you run a free seminar for prospects, there is often an unspoken assumption that while you will give away some interesting information, your seminar will also be a sales pitch. I attended a breakfast seminar sponsored by Microsoft and the Yellow Pages, and running throughout all the presentations was the underlying theme of 'what we can do for you'. Another free seminar I went to was hosted by an email marketing company, which included slides in its presentation of what great results it had achieved for its clients. This blatant self-promotion seemed reasonable at a free seminar, but I wouldn't have felt the same way had I paid for either event.

If you're running a free event for prospects, rather than for clients or customers, you have to be realistic about the number of 'no shows' on the day. People feel a stronger commitment to attend events they've paid for or when they have a relationship with you. Prospects don't have anything to lose by not turning up and they'll often make that decision at the last moment and won't bother letting you know. You can minimise the risk of 'no shows' by sending personal invitations and keeping your numbers small.

If you do decide to run free seminars, one way of reducing the costs and time involved is to run a seminar with another related small business. For example, an email marketing agency could partner with a law firm to talk about privacy and spam issues.

You may decide you want to charge a fee for your seminars to either cover your costs or make a profit. Such seminars then

John Pettit runs seasonal seminars in each city with the idea of promoting new-season plants. He started these seminars two years ago and after a slow start they're now proving very popular and there's usually a waiting list. Initially the seminars were free, but John found he had too many 'no shows' so now he charges a minimal fee to cover the costs.

The seminars are held from 9.30 a.m. to 12 noon on a Sunday. Coffee, tea and cakes are served on arrival, and the formal session starts at 10 a.m. once everyone has had time to mingle and wander through the nursery.

The format is the same each time. John invites a guest speaker who talks about specific plants, such as spring bulbs. Then John gives some gardening tips for the season and demonstrates skills, such as pruning or making compost. Wherever possible, he involves the participants. For example, if he's demonstrating how to re-pot plants, everyone will have a small pot plant to practise with.

At the end of the seminar, participants receive a free plant and can purchase other plants at a 15 per cent discount.

become part of your business as well as a marketing tool. The advantages of charging for seminars are that you then attract people who are genuinely interested in attending and you will know with more certainty what size room to hire and how many people to cater for.

If you charge, you can encourage participants to register early by providing an early bird discount. This is a two-edged sword though, as in my experience people either register early or at the last minute and if you have an early bird discount, you risk losing the last-minute registrations.

Deciding how much to charge is often difficult. One way of getting a feel for prices is to find out how much your competitors charge. Then look at who you want to come to your seminars and what you think they will realistically pay. If your

---

*Blue Gum*
RESTAURANT

Tania James and Bill Johnson run three cooking seminars each year. The aim of these seminars is to get to know their corporate clients and prospects better and give something back to their regular customers. The cooking seminars are free and by invitation only. They've been running these seminars for 18 months and the word is getting out. Customers are now asking to be invited.

Tania and Bill also run breakfast seminars for Mother's Day and Father's Day and occasionally for other events. After the cooking lesson is over, the staff and guests sit down to enjoy a gourmet champagne breakfast.

Although Tania and Bill charge for the seminars they run they regard them as largely promotional because by the time they take out their costs, including the expense of advertising in the local newspapers, they don't make much profit.

**Jane Amos**
NATURAL THERAPIST

Once a year, Jane Amos joins with two colleagues—a beauty therapist and a clairvoyant—to run a one-day 'Pamper Yourself' seminar.

The main aim of the seminar is to build their profiles in the community. Jane, the beauty therapist and the clairvoyant all give presentations about their professions and then offer short individual sessions. The presentations are free, but they charge a minimal fee for the individual sessions, partly to limit the numbers and also to cover their overheads, which include hiring a facility and paying a friend to sit at the door to take bookings for them.

Jane also hands out her brochure to everyone who attends and gives them a coupon offering a 25 per cent discount on their next appointment.

seminars are too cheap, you may not appear professional enough for your target market, and if they're too expensive they might be out of reach of the people you want to attend.

## Types of seminars

Traditional seminars are held in a physical location, but today you can also run web seminars (often called webinars), and telephone seminars (usually called teleseminars).

### The traditional live seminar

Traditional seminars are held in a physical venue—either your office or in a hotel or function venue. The number of participants varies. Some seminars are large, catering for hundreds, while others are small and intimate.

The advantage of live seminars is that they are very personal and you can have in-depth conversations with customers, clients and prospects who will see you in a different context, learn something new, and gain a greater understanding of your capabilities. This experience will often increase their trust and confidence in your business and make it easier for you to follow up naturally after the event.

The disadvantages are the costs of hiring a room and catering, the time it takes to organise an event, and the uncertainty surrounding any event organisation. It's often impossible to predict how successful an event will be, and attendance can be fickle for no apparent reason. Monitoring and measuring your results over a period of time is the only way to tell whether you're getting a return on your investment.

SMALL SEMINARS FOR PROFESSIONAL SERVICES

In *Managing the Professional Services Firm,* David H. Maister (1997, pp. 121–4) gives some guidelines on how professional firms can have highly individualised face-to-face dialogue with prospects at seminars. He says:

> Since the essence of getting hired is getting a specific individual client to talk about his or her problems, the sooner you can commence the dialogue, the better the tactic. Professional services are not a 'mass' business—clients are acquired one at a time, and any marketing program must reflect this.

Maister stresses that the seminar numbers must be kept low (a maximum of 25 participants) as it is better to give a lot of attention to a small, select audience than pay a little attention to a large number of prospects. He says once your prospects have accepted your invitation, you must conduct thorough research on each company and person attending and compile a briefing document for the staff member sitting next to the guest. He advises not to scrimp on this research as the more you know about each company, the more comfortable they'll feel talking about their business and problems.

Maister recommends that the seating is random. You must assign one partner or staff member to sit with five prospects. The partner or staff member converses with these prospects, making it known they've done their homework by asking relevant questions about each of their businesses. With this opening, even before the presentation has started, your prospect will start to realise you're enterprising, disciplined and organised, have done your homework, are interested in their business, and are willing to invest in the relationship.

The seminar presenter speaks for 20–30 minutes, then Maister suggests breaking up into small group discussions. The seminar proceeds in this fashion: 20-minute presentation, 20-minute discussion, then back to the speaker again. This structure maximises the opportunity for individual dialogue and gives your prospects a chance to talk comfortably about their issues.

The follow-up after the seminar is now easier as the partner or staff member who sat next to the five prospects can ring them and have a personal conversation carrying on from where they left off at the seminar. They may even do some more research on a topic they were discussing before they ring so they have new information to offer.

## Webinars

Webinars (web seminars) are live seminars conducted using the Internet. Your webinar is open to anyone, irrespective of where they live, as long as the time suits them. Most are short—about 90 minutes. Participants watching a webinar see the presenter, PowerPoint presentations and pages from websites.

Most webinars are interactive, with participants asking questions through their microphones or as text. Some presenters use a polling feature which allows them to ask questions and participants to respond. A few presenters will take questions during the presentation, but most talk first and then take questions at the end or during regular Q&A breaks.

Many presenters make hand-outs of the PowerPoint slides available to participants to download. Others make a CD or Flash file of the webinar available for both participants and those who were unable to attend.

As with live seminars, some webinars are free and others charge a fee. You need to have a large database to make webinars work for you as only a small percentage of those you invite will participate.

One way of attracting attendees is to have a big-name presenter. Selecting someone outside your organisation will also add credence to the value of the event as your webinar will not be regarded as an infomercial. Many people think big-name presenters are hard to get, but that may not be the case. Sometimes you may have to pay them, but if you tell them about the amount of free publicity they'll receive and the exposure they'll get to their target market, they may reduce their fee or do it for nothing.

## Teleseminars

Teleseminars are similar to webinars in many ways, except that the information is conveyed over the phone, not online, so there are no visual elements to the presentation. As with webinars, listeners stay in their own home or office, or join with other people in a central location.

A common format is for the speaker to make their presentation and then ask for questions. Often the organisers will email presentation notes to participants beforehand so they can follow these notes as they listen.

With a webinar, your main costs are in the initial set-up, but with teleseminars you have to rent a bridge line for each seminar. Most companies charge according to the number of people you expect to call. The cost also varies depending on the length of your event, whether you want an operator to assist you, and if you want a tape, CD or transcript of the teleseminar. If you do teleseminars regularly, you may save by paying a flat monthly rental fee.

## Advantages of teleseminars and webinars

Teleseminars and webinars raise your profile as an expert in your field. They are particularly useful if you want to gain an international reputation and sell products over your website to a global market. You can make a handsome profit by selling large numbers of reasonably priced products, such as books, CDs and tapes.

After the initial cost of the technology to organise and run teleseminars and webinars, they are cheaper and less time-consuming to organise than traditional seminars. Registration, payment, attendance management and post-event reporting can all be done via the Internet.

If you're running teleseminars and webinars as a profit-making venture as well as a marketing tool, you can also charge for a CD or transcript of the event. You can continue to sell the CD for a long time after the actual event. Viral marketing—

online word-of-mouth through people forwarding emails to friends and colleagues—may also increase sales.

## Disadvantages of teleseminars and webinars

Teleseminars and webinars don't allow for personal conversations apart from the public Q&A sessions. A lot of the people who attend your webinars are never likely to be your customers or clients unless they buy your products online.

Webinars do not provide a networking occasion for participants, unless they join with others to watch or listen to the presentation. A few teleseminars or webinars, with the permission of the participants, make the names and contact details of the participants available to all attendees, but I'm not sure how many people would contact each other after such a presentation.

### Case study

A MarketingSherpa e-newsletter (2004) talks about American public relations consultant Annie Jennings, who runs free teleseminars to gain new business. Unlike many public relations firms, Annie only charges for resulting media placements. Until she discovered teleseminars, most of her new business came through word of mouth, but she found there was a natural limit to relying on referrals.

After two years of running regular teleseminars, Annie's client list has expanded dramatically. The teleseminars have also taken on a life of their own and Annie has expanded the program from fortnightly to two or three times a week.

Annie researched the technology before she started and then decided on her content and format. She chooses business topics relevant to her

> clients and prospects and often invites guest speakers to talk about subjects she's not an expert in.
>
> Annie decided that the standard lecture format wouldn't work as people would get bored, so she chose an interview format. To provide even more variety, she hired another interviewer as a co-moderator and, like duos on breakfast radio shows, they spark off each other. The dual interviewing format gives the teleseminar more personality, tone and overall branding than a series of guest speakers would.
>
> She launched an e-newsletter to market her teleseminars and offered free tapes after the event as a way of lead generation, goodwill and branding. Every tape mailed out includes her brochure. On average, about half the people who sign up for an event request the tape afterwards.

## Planning your seminars

Many people when they start out have unrealistic expectations about how many people will attend their seminars. Only a small percentage of the people you reach will attend, so unless you have a large database or a speaker that people will queue to listen to, plan for small numbers and advertise that there will be limited places.

If you are running a series of seminars, put them in your diary for a year ahead so you can organise them well in advance. When choosing dates, try to avoid school holidays and public holidays, such as Easter, that could affect attendance. Opinion varies on how far in advance you should promote your seminars. Some say the more advance information you give people the better, while others contend that attending a short seminar is a spontaneous decision, so leave promotion to a few weeks beforehand. In my observation, seminars tend to be most heavily promoted about six weeks in advance.

Choose a day of the week that will appeal to your target audience. Most seminars are held on Tuesday, Wednesday or Thursday, but if you know a Monday or Friday will suit your customers and prospects, hold your event on those days. If you have a major client who you want to attend, check what date suits them.

The length of your seminar will depend on your topic and audience, but most free seminars seem to last between 90 minutes and three hours. Make sure you finish on time or people will start leaving early, which is disconcerting for your speakers.

Choose a time of day that suits you and your target audience. Many seminars are held first thing in the morning or in the early evening. The advantage of a breakfast seminar is that you catch people before they get caught up in their day. The advantage of an early evening event is that they are more relaxed, no longer worrying about what they have to do that day.

If it isn't practical to hold a seminar in your own office, you'll need to hire a venue. Spend some time researching possible venues, as room prices vary considerably. Also consider the location in terms of distance from your major customers, clients and prospects, as parking and proximity to bus and train stops can be issues. You need to make attending as easy as possible, so include a location map in your invitation.

Even if your seminar is free, ask people to make a reservation so you know how many to cater for. Allow for 10–15 per cent 'no shows' at free events. You can set up an online registration system to make registrations more efficient. Then send or email a confirmation form with details on how to get to the seminar. Send a reminder email a couple of days before the event.

# Your presentation

You'll often be the person making the presentation, but if you invite speakers to join you, check them out if you haven't heard them before as it's your reputation on the line as much as theirs. Liking people is no guarantee that you can work well with them.

Remember that people learn in different ways—kinaesthetic learners learn through smell, taste, feeling, sensing and touch; visual learners like reading, writing, watching videos or looking at slides; and auditory learners like listening, discussing and talking.

You may not be able to cater for all ways of learning in your presentation, but you may be able to combine several methods to suit various learners, for example workbooks or hand-outs, overhead transparencies, flipcharts with pre-prepared or blank pages, props, samples, slides, a PowerPoint presentation or even videos. And don't forget that *you* are also a visual aid, as people will watch the way you move and gesture.

The PowerPoint presentation is probably the most used and abused form of visual presentation in seminars. The best PowerPoint slides are clear and easy to read. Make your design simple and in keeping with your brand. Avoid the common mistakes of putting too much information on each slide, displaying graphs and diagrams that are impossible to read, and using too many different colours.

Many presenters hand out a copy of their PowerPoint presentation with ruled lines alongside each slide for people to write their own notes. You can make your notes a more valuable resource by using the 'notes' function in PowerPoint to record additional information for each slide.

## Start strongly

First impressions count, so whatever way you introduce your seminar, you need to grab the audience's attention and let them know what they can expect out of your topic. If the group is small, you could ask them to introduce themselves and state what they want to get out of the seminar. This may seem a slow way to start, but it is useful if you want an interactive seminar with group discussions.

Alternatively, you could begin with a story or by giving a brief outline of the topic and stating what benefits your audience will receive from your presentation.

John Pettit gives seminars on growing vegetables and herbs in inner-city gardens. He starts like this:

> Through the years, many people have asked me what made me interested in gardening. Like many of you, I grew up in suburbia and my mother was a keen gardener. I learnt to appreciate the taste of homegrown vegetables. I now live in an inner-city apartment, but I want to continue to enjoy eating vegetables straight from the garden. Even when you'll be able to buy sandwiches that can last two years or chemically synthesised food, nothing will be able to beat homegrown tomatoes with that taste of yesteryear.
>
> This morning I'm going to show you how to grow tomatoes in small spaces. You'll also be able to use these techniques to grow other vegetables and herbs. First, I'll take you through an overview. Then we'll break down each step in the process. I'll demonstrate and there will be time for you to practise.

> At the end of the seminar, you'll each have planted a tomato plant to take home. These tomato plants, if cared for properly, should each produce at least 50 delicious tomatoes.
>
> The methods I'm teaching you are based on my 30 years' experience in gardening. I can vouch for the quality of the tomato plants as they're from my own stock. Perhaps the greatest advocate I have of these tomato plants is a friend of mine: she hates gardening but having tasted these tomatoes, she now grows them on her apartment windowsill.
>
> So get comfortable and let me show you how to grow the best tomatoes you've ever tasted.

## Make your evaluation forms useful

Consider whether to have an evaluation form as part of your seminar and, if so, what questions you'll ask (see Figure 7.1). The greatest value of evaluation forms is receiving constructive criticism on how you can improve your content or delivery. Often, you will already know how you can improve, but occasionally you'll receive an idea you hadn't thought of.

Take the feedback seriously, but not personally as the comments are only snapshots of how people feel at the time, not an indication of what they have learnt. And often the evaluations say more about the people filling them out than they do about you, the presenter.

Most evaluation forms have a number of tick boxes and also spaces for people to make comments if they want to. Names are usually optional. You can make your evaluation form more useful by asking people how they would describe your seminar if they were recommending it to other people. The responses

**Figure 7.1 Evaluation form for the 'Pamper Yourself' *seminar***

***Evaluation of the natural therapies seminar content*** Please tick (✓) appropriate box

1. How well did the seminar meet its stated objectives?

   ☐ EXCELLENT  ☐ ABOVE AVERAGE  ☐ AVERAGE  ☐ BELOW AVERAGE  ☐ POOR

   What aspects of the seminar did you find most helpful?
   _____
   _____

   Suggestions to improve the seminar content or structure:
   _____
   _____

2. Evaluation of the presentation style

   How effective was the presenter's style (e.g. mix of theory, practice and discussion)?

   ☐ EXCELLENT  ☐ ABOVE AVERAGE  ☐ AVERAGE  ☐ BELOW AVERAGE  ☐ POOR

   Comments:
   _____
   _____

3. Overall evaluation

   ☐ EXCELLENT  ☐ ABOVE AVERAGE  ☐ AVERAGE  ☐ BELOW AVERAGE  ☐ POOR

   Additional comments:
   _____
   _____

4. What will you take away from the seminar and apply to your own life?
   _____
   _____

5. How would you describe this seminar if you were recommending it to other people?
   _____
   _____

6. Would you like to receive Jane Amos's natural therapy monthly e-newsletter?

   ☐ YES    ☐ NO

7. Would you like to receive occasional emails about other seminars?

   ☐ YES    ☐ NO

   Thank you

will be useful for future marketing material. You can also ask them for their email address if they would like to subscribe to your e-newsletter or receive emails about other seminars.

## Promote your seminars

Although seminars are a promotional tool, you need to promote them to get bums on seats, especially when you're starting out and your seminars aren't well known. Plan what promotion methods to use and how many reminders you will send. A rule of thumb is the shorter the event, the shorter the marketing time.

Common marketing methods are flyers, emails, ads, press releases or personalised invitations. You can test different methods on different events to see what works best for you. Whatever methods you use, your marketing material needs to be distinctive and in keeping with your brand. You need an informative catchy title and a few brief paragraphs that sum up the content. You also need brief bios on the presenters, preferably with photos.

### Personalised invitations

A personalised invitation is likely to get the greatest response rate, but will narrow your range of attendees. It's ideal for small, tailored seminars. A print invitation is also a bit of a novelty these days with so much business conducted by email.

### Email invitations

Email invitations are convenient as people can register online immediately if you provide a hyperlink to a landing page on your website. You may want to offer an inducement to register, such as the first five people to register receiving a small prize. If you're sending email invitations, only send emails to people who've given you permission to do so. Otherwise your email will just be spam.

## Press releases

You may have difficulty getting a general press release about a seminar published unless you find a newsworthy angle, have a link to a current news story, or have a good relationship with your local newspaper. However, many local newspapers have online and offline calendar-of-events sections that will promote your seminars. If appropriate for the audience you are targeting, you can also send your press release to alternative free newspapers, such as art-related or new-age tabloids.

## Radio

Don't overlook radio as a promotion method. Contact the program manager at your local radio station and offer yourself as a guest. Once on air, talk on your area of expertise and ask the host to mention your upcoming seminar.

## Community help

Ask associations you belong to, such as your local chamber of commerce, and even competitors with e-newsletters, if they will promote your seminar for you. Often, competitors will be willing to give your event a plug. Sometimes they may ask for a small fee, but more often they'll do it for nothing.

You can put flyers on noticeboards in the community in places such as clubs and health food shops. You could also consider doing a letterbox drop.

### Delite Landscape DESIGN

John Pettit promotes his seasonal seminars in his e-newsletters, on his website, on billboards outside his shops, and in ads in the local papers. He also sends a press release to the local paper and offers a free place to each paper. As these seasonal seminars are regular events, he now has a loyal group who attend each one and word of mouth has helped build attendance.

People can book on his website, over the phone or in his shops. All reservations are entered into the website so staff know how many are attending.

### Blue Gum RESTAURANT

Tania James and Bill Johnson promote special-occasion cooking classes (Father's Day and Mother's Day) on their website, on the back of their menu and in their e-newsletter. They also have a monthly business card draw for new subscribers to their e-newsletter and offer the winner a free place at the next cooking seminar. They send a press release to the local newspapers and are talking to one local paper about writing a monthly recipe column.

One of the main attractions of their cooking seminars is the quality of the chefs. Blue Gum Restaurant's chef always invites another chef to join him. Having different contributing chefs encourages many participants to come again next time.

By joining forces with two colleagues, Jane is able to share the cost of the marketing for the 'Pamper Yourself' seminars. They placed an ad in the local newspapers, put flyers up in health food stores, pre-schools and doctors' rooms, invited the lifestyle editor from a Sunday paper to attend, promoted the seminar on their websites and in their e-newsletters, and asked all their colleagues to spread the word. They had an overwhelming response.

# Get extra mileage out of your seminar

Everyone who comes to your seminars needs to walk away with something to remember you by. Your phone number needs to be handy when they decide they want your products or services. So give everyone who attends something to walk away with. This may be a folder with a copy of the presentation notes, some material about your business, your business card, or a small gift, such as a pen with your name and logo on it.

Use the best of the comments on the evaluation forms as testimonials if the person has given their permission. If all the evaluations are anonymous, ring a few people and ask for testimonials. Most people, in my experience, are happy to write a few words you can use on your website or other promotional material.

Find a way of following up with participants after the event. For example, you could email them a copy of the presentation notes or just thank them for attending. Make sure they all know about the next seminar you're planning before they leave, so they can put it in their diaries and spread the word to their colleagues.

Consider using the seminar material in other ways. If you've recorded it, you could give it away or sell the tape or CD over your website. Or you could turn the material into an article and post it on your website or include it in your e-newsletter. To get even greater mileage, you could also send your article to other websites that take free articles.

## Are your seminars helping you to talk up your business?

Keep a database on everyone who attends your seminars and over a period of time, you will be able to track how much new and repeat business you gain from your seminars. It's harder to measure the effect on your reputation, but you will get a feel for whether seminars are helping your business from the feedback you receive both at and after each event.

John Pettit finds his nurseries consistently sell more new-season stock the week after his seminars, but this is partly because he advertises to promote the seminars. Irrespective of the increased sales, he thinks the seminars are worth doing as he's building a loyal group of customers who now choose his nursery over his competitors'.

## Blue Gum RESTAURANT

The use of Blue Gum's corporate function room has increased by 24 per cent over the last year, which Tania James and Bill Johnson attribute to the relationships they're building with their seminar series. They now know several human resources managers well and enjoy working with them.

## Jane Amos NATURAL THERAPIST

Although the organisation of the 'Pamper Yourself' seminar took more time than she anticipated, Jane was delighted with the results.

As she works on her own, Jane enjoyed the experience of working with colleagues. Running the seminar increased her self-confidence and she also gained several ongoing clients.

# 8  More ways to talk up your business

There are many more creative ways to talk up your business, such as donating prizes at networking events or participating in a street festival. Often, you'll come up with these ideas yourself, or someone will approach you with an idea. But sometimes it helps to sit down with a group of friends or colleagues and brainstorm ideas. Many of the ideas will be unrealistic, but there may be some gems.

## Become involved in your community

If your business is an integral part of the local community, see how you can become involved in community events and at the same time get some free publicity. For example, you might donate some books to a school library or take part in a local debate.

As well as participating in existing events, you could create a separate promotion to coincide with a local event. For example, if you were a personal fitness coach, you could promote your training before a local marathon race. Alternatively, you could become a sponsor so your name appears on all the event's promotional material.

### Delite Landscape DESIGN

Every year John Pettit donates plants to local primary schools for the students to plant on Plant a Tree Day. The children plant some of these trees in the schools and plant others in the community, in places such as retirement villages and streets with no trees.

In exchange for this donation, Delite Landscape Design is recognised in the school newsletter which goes to all parents. John also puts banners outside the schools on the day they plant the trees. Often, the local newspaper sends a reporter to cover the event.

### Blue Gum RESTAURANT

Blue Gum Restaurant takes part in a local street fair once a year and Tania James and Bill Johnson set up a table outside the restaurant and sell gourmet snacks. All the shop owners participating in the street fair contribute to the costs of the flyers which are put in neighbourhood letterboxes. The street committee also places ads in the local newspapers. The gala day attracts some sponsorship and the local paper always runs an article the following week.

Tania and Bill find the bookings at their restaurant are high the week after the street festival.

>
> **Jane Amos**
> NATURAL THERAPIST
>
> Jane Amos does reiki treatments at franchise association conferences held in a local hotel. The conference organisers share the proceeds from her treatments. In exchange, Jane puts up her billboard on the day, hands out brochures and is given a free advertisement in the association's next newsletter.

## Sponsorship

According to IEG, Inc. (www.sponsorship.com)—a major provider of sponsorship research—sponsorship has been the fastest growing form of marketing over the past decade. IEG estimates worldwide sponsorship at $28 billion in 2004, a rise of 8.1 per cent from $25.9 billion in 2003.

In the past, sponsorship was limited to fairly traditional areas, such as sports and the arts, but today the range of events and organisations that are sponsored is much wider. You can choose events and organisations as diverse as dog shows and speaking organisations. One of the great advantages of sponsoring an event or organisation is that you can reach your target market without having to organise the promotion yourself and you may gain greater reach and exposure than from an advertisement.

Before selecting an organisation to sponsor, ask yourself what you want to achieve with your sponsorship and how much money and time you are willing to give. You also need to factor in how much money you will spend to gain the maximum benefit from your sponsorship. Often, exploiting the sponsorship will cost you as much, if not more, than the initial investment.

Sometimes you can become a sponsor by donating your time or a product rather than giving money. For example, a designer might give an organisation free design services for a specified number of hours in exchange for sponsorship. Or a speaker might give an organisation some copies of their CD or book.

Make sure you select a company or organisation that reflects your values and supports your branding so your business will benefit from the images and associations attached to them. Also ask yourself whether there are any risks associated with this partnership and what impact those risks could have on your image. For example, if you sponsor a football team and they go on a drunken rampage through the local school, would this affect your image?

## Do your research first

Examine an event or company's track record before deciding whether or not to sponsor them. If the event is new, make sure the organiser is reputable and experienced. Find out details about the average attendance and attendees' demographic profiles. The more information you have, the better you'll be able to judge whether the sponsorship suits your brand and will grow your business.

As well as getting the statistics, talk to some of the event's existing sponsors. Ask them what they like and dislike about the event and what they get out of their sponsorship. Often, an event may have an existing sponsorship package, but these can sometimes be tailored to suit your needs. For example, instead of free tickets you could ask for a larger ad in the event program. Once you've agreed on the sponsorship package, get it in writing so there's no room for disagreement later.

Discuss with the event organiser how the event will be marketed and see if there are any additional promotional opportunities for you, such as putting up your own billboard or offering a gift to the first people who register.

John Pettit sponsors a number of associations' conferences by providing large pot plant arrangements on the stage and in break-out conference rooms. He also donates plants for the conference convenors to give as gifts to members of their organising committees.

In exchange, Delite Landscape Design is mentioned in the conference promotional material and thanked during the conferences. John has found that many associations have subsequently become clients, buying pot plants for their offices.

Tania James and Bill Johnson sponsor their son's soccer team, largely to give something back to the sport their son has played since he was five. The restaurant's name goes on the newsletter and it can display a banner at team events.

## Trade shows

Trade shows bring together businesses, suppliers, customers and media representatives in a given industry. They are usually held over several days and people wander through viewing or buying the products at the different stalls. Often stalls will host entertainment and invite special guests to join them.

Almost every industry has trade shows and many businesses feel they have to attend to maintain a presence. If they're not there, their competitors or customers might wonder why and think the worst—have they sold their business, retired or gone broke?

Although not cheap, trade shows are also a way of meeting prospects, maintaining customer or client contact, introducing new products to your market, developing media relations, and staying on top of what's happening in your field. If you intend making trade shows a regular part of your marketing, it's worth investing in a professionally designed booth that reflects your image and brand.

If your industry has more than one show, do your research to see which one would be most beneficial for you. Ask questions like: How many stalls were there last year? How many people visited the show? Who's sponsoring the event?

Working a trade show booth is exhausting and you will need other people to help you staff the booth. Set up shifts of three or four hours each, and give everyone time to take breaks away from the booth. A study in 2004 by the Center for Exhibition Industry Research (CEIR) found companies that train their staff in exhibiting goals and qualifying and closing techniques reported the greatest increase in the number of quality leads they gathered.

Evaluate your success after the show. Did you reach your goals? Did your show reach the right audience? Note your successes and brainstorm how to do better next time.

### Tips on how to get greater mileage out of your trade shows

- Let your customers, clients and prospects know that you'll be exhibiting at the trade show and where they can find you. Issue this invitation by letter, email or phone.

- Find out what media are attending and make appointments with them before you arrive at the show.
- Train your staff well. Make sure they wear business identification or a uniform. Ask your staff to visit all the other stalls as well as work on your own to see what your competitors are offering.
- Have a means of collecting names for follow up after the show—for example, a raffle or lucky door prize—and send a letter or gift to prospects who took the time to fill out your forms at the trade show.
- If you decide to give away promotional gifts, make sure they stand out as most people's show bags will go straight into the bin afterwards.

John Pettit feels he can't afford to miss the leading annual national gardening trade show. His presence indicates his business is still a leading player in the market and he learns what his competitors are doing. He views taking a stall as an investment rather than a marketing tool as he seldom gains much business directly out of trade shows.

# Run your own conference

If you're one of the leaders in your field, instead of attending a trade show, you could run your own conference (see Chapter 7). You may not make a profit from this venture, but if you choose good speakers and make your conference a 'must attend' event, you'll receive great publicity. If organising conferences seems daunting, hire a professional conference organiser to arrange it for you.

## Find yourself a radio or TV spot or write a regular column

Many experts find themselves a regular radio or TV spot, where they talk about their topic and answer listeners' queries. For example, a business coach may have a regular spot on a radio station and talk about how small businesses can market themselves on a limited budget.

Even if you can't find yourself a regular radio or TV spot, you may be able to secure the occasional appearance on small business programs. Many of these are radio or TV programs, but some magazines also have a CD and some airlines have an audio program. Sometimes you may be approached because of your reputation, but you can make the initial approach. Writing articles for magazines or the Internet is another way of establishing your expertise. I've been interviewed twice about e-newsletters thanks to two articles I've written on the subject.

Many small business owners also write a regular column for a newspaper or magazine. Some are paid for writing a column and others do it for nothing in exchange for the publicity they receive.

*Blue Gum*
RESTAURANT

Bill Johnson is interviewed occasionally on radio programs about how to survive a family business. He and Tania James are currently negotiating to write a regular recipe column in the local newspaper.

John Pettit has a regular spot on a radio program. He gives some gardening tips and then answers listeners' questions about design and gardening problems. He also appears regularly as a guest on the TV program *Gardening for the 21st Century*.

After Jane Amos and her colleagues ran their 'Pamper Yourself' seminar, she was interviewed by the local radio station about relaxation methods for busy people. Jane has recently started writing a regular column in her local newspaper about managing the 'overwhelm' factor when you're a working mother.

## Stand out in a crowd

Some people create a unique clothing style and make it part of their branding. For example, you may decide to always wear bright pink—bright pink lipstick, nail polish, suit, tie, scarf, tie pin or shirt. People start to remember you—and talk about you—because of the clothes you wear.

Even if you don't do something as dramatic as dress in pink, your clothes must suit the brand you stand for. If you need help creating a memorable personal image, consult an image consultant.

# Train your staff to provide great customer service

The way you treat your clients and customers at all stages of the buying process will influence your word-of-mouth reputation and repeat business. Train your staff to dress, speak and act in accordance with your brand. It's often the little things that matter: how promptly your staff serve your customers, whether or not they smile, and how they handle difficult customers.

After John Pettit learnt from his customer survey that some customers were dissatisfied as they had to wait too long for service, he employed more casual staff for the peak hours and also trained his staff to be more efficient. This training drew on ideas provided by the staff.

*Blue Gum* RESTAURANT

Aware that branding is so important for their image, Tania James and Bill Johnson have decided it's time to redesign their staff uniforms. As they want their staff to wear the uniform with pride, they are including them in the discussions with the designer.

# Partner with complementary associates or businesses

If you're a sole trader or small business working on your own, you can get stuck in a rut. Joining forces with a complementary business or associate can help you grow your business faster as you'll pool your resources and databases. You'll also motivate each other to achieve more.

Some examples of complementary businesses are a make-up artist working with a photographer, a graphic designer working with a printer, and a business coach partnering with an image consultant.

# 9 Grow your business from within

**B**usiness growth occurs in cycles, similar to sharemarket waves. When business is booming, you run to keep up with all your orders. In quiet times, some business owners feel despondent and wonder when the next big wave is coming.

Use these quiet times to prepare your business for the busy times. If your business is not in good shape internally, your business systems won't cope well when you're inundated with work. So you'll go from worrying about where the next job is coming from, to lying awake at night worrying about how you're going to cope with all your work. Develop your personal skills and create business systems to get you through both the boom and lean times.

A sense of entrepreneurship got you into your business. What personal skills and systems will help you grow your business?

## Persist with a purpose and patience

Read about any successful businessperson and you'll find that most 'overnight success stories' are preceded by years of hard work. Having a vision or a dream, working hard, and persisting against the odds are common themes. Successful businesspeople don't just talk about their ideas; they put their plans into action. I recently redid my marketing plan and was reminded that while I was clear about my goals, I needed to action each step to achieve them.

Many successful businesspeople also fail more often than most other people, but they pick themselves up after these failures and try again. For example, Dr Seuss's first children's book was rejected by 23 publishers, Abraham Lincoln failed in business and lost several elections, and it took Henry Ford three attempts to set up his own motor company.

Sometimes, persistence also requires patience and trust. Your latest business idea may not fail dramatically, but nor may it take off in the way—or at the speed—you expect. Often, you can understand *why* in retrospect—maybe the time wasn't right, maybe you were targeting the wrong market, or maybe the product or service needed further refining. But at the time it feels like you are trying to push back the petals on a bud before the flower is ready to open.

When you're in such a 'no-go' period, sometimes the hardest but sanest thing to do is to make sure you've done all you possibly can, then let the idea go for a while, and trust. If the idea is right, when you come back to it your actions will flow and you will no longer feel like you're pushing an immovable object. At other times, persistence may be the key and you may succeed by slowly and steadily chipping away until you make a breakthrough.

## Continual improvement

You need to gain new knowledge and learn new skills continually to keep up with changes in your industry and stay motivated about your business. If you're comfortable and complacent, it's often a sign you're stagnating and at this point, having a 'regular' job may start to seem an attractive option.

You always have to be aware of what your competitors are doing and what's happening in the marketplace. If you see the early signs of change, you can adapt your business before your competitors do so. For example, the advent of the Internet meant many writers and designers had to adapt their print skills to a new medium. Or if your business is dependent on outsourced work from a large corporation, and you see the signs that the corporation is planning to take work back in-house, you can diversify your business to minimise the impact.

You can stay abreast of current trends in your marketplace by reading industry trade magazines and e-newsletters. You can also interview your current customers and clients to find out what's happening in their field. One way of doing this is to do an online survey, but you often learn more by conducting personal interviews with about five people—in person or over the phone. You may receive the most useful answers from open-ended questions, which give the person room to express their thoughts and feelings. For example, you could ask: 'What work issues keep you awake at 3 a.m.?' or 'What do you think are the greatest changes happening in your industry?'

Another way of keeping up in your field and improving your credibility is to gain formal qualifications or accreditation. For example, a person training in ethical sales might do a graduate degree in ethics, a public speaker might become a CSP (Credited

Speaking Professional), and a manufacturer might get ISO accreditation for a product.

At other times, short training courses, such as day or evening workshops, may be enough to give your skills a boost. For example, although I spent a few years in Toastmasters and have

### Delite Landscape DESIGN

John Pettit has hired a business coach for a three-month period to help him improve his public speaking skills. This coaching is concentrating on three elements of presentation: structure, developing material and delivery.

### Blue Gum RESTAURANT

Tania James and Bill Johnson sent their chef on a one-week refresher course and hired a locum to replace him while he was away. Tania has also enrolled for a one-year online restaurant management certificate.

###  Jane Amos NATURAL THERAPIST

Jane Amos's work is always quiet during the summer holidays, so she decided to use this time productively by doing a 10-day kinesiology course. Jane has had an interest in kinesiology for a while as she's read it links traditional Chinese acupuncture with Western healing methods. The course outline promised to teach her the techniques of manual muscle testing for energy balancing.

made several public speeches, when I dropped out of public speaking for about 18 months I was surprised to find that the thought of public speaking seemed daunting. So I attended a couple of workshops to brush up my skills.

## Learn from your experience

Often, your successes come from learning from your experiences. Looking back on what you've done—what went well and what failed—will help you improve your products and services, as well as your processes. You can debrief on your own, with your staff, with clients or customers, and with your peers.

Debriefing by yourself is valuable as you'll admit failures you may not admit to other people. You'll probably be your harshest critic, so remember you'll learn more and move on faster if you acknowledge your mistakes but are not too hard on yourself.

Debriefing with your staff has the advantage of making them feel involved and also offers you more than one perspective on the same situation.

Debriefing with the client or customer helps improve your skills and develops a deeper relationship with them. They may be willing to describe the buying process from their point of view and tell you how you can improve your product or service.

Debriefing with peers often encourages you to look at other ways of doing things in the future.

## Find yourself a coach or mentor

Many successful businesspeople have a coach or mentor to bounce ideas around with. A professional coach is sometimes better to talk to about business than a friend as they don't have preconceived ideas about you and they listen rather than trying to tell you about their similar experiences. A coach can often help you clarify your thoughts when you're going over and over something in your mind.

But coaches are more than 'paid listeners'. It's easy to get caught up in the day-to-day operations of your business and not see the bigger picture. A coach can help you develop business strategies and keep you accountable for implementing them.

## Create an advisory board

Some small businesses create themselves an advisory board composed of people who are genuinely interested in seeing their business prosper. The value of an advisory board is that you receive expert advice and ideas. Make it clear when you approach your board members that you're not asking for a lot of their time—many advisory boards only meet quarterly. You can either pay them for their time or host a lunch or dinner for the meeting.

You only need two or three people on your advisory board. Choose people you admire, such as other businesspeople or retired businesspeople. Prepare a report and agenda for each meeting and distribute them ahead of time. Be honest with your advisory board so you get the full benefit of their management expertise.

A novel idea I read about recently is to create an imaginary advisory board. Once again choose people you respect—either living or dead—and consult them when you need advice. For example, if you need expert advice on management issues, you could have an imaginary conversation with Tom Peters, author of *In Search of Excellence* (1982) and *The Brand You* (1999). If you want an opinion on what to wear, you could 'ask' Audrey Hepburn or Madonna, depending on your personal style.

John Pettit has just signed up for a business coaching program which covers leadership, marketing, finance, management, lead generation, lead conversion and client fulfilment. These seven skills are taught through training modules, audio tapes and workbooks, and individual coaching is provided by phone and email.

Through this course, John hopes to start planning for when he exits his business. He would like to sell two branches in a few years, then ease out of the remaining one slowly, maintaining a less active role in the business.

Tania James and Bill Johnson recently formed an advisory board that meets quarterly over dinner at Blue Gum Restaurant. Their board members are two retired restaurant owners and a friend who runs his own self-storage business. They pay the board members a small retainer and provide the meal.

### Jane Amos
### NATURAL THERAPIST

Jane Amos has a personal coach whom she talks to over the phone for an hour every two weeks. Although an expensive item in Jane's budget, she thinks she receives great value from this coaching. Sometimes, because she works on her own, Jane finds she loses sight of her goals, and she gets bogged down by administrative details or the occasional ungrateful client. Talking to her personal coach helps Jane keep a better sense of perspective about her business.

# Staffing

One of the best ways to keep staff loyal is to involve them in your business. You can make people feel they are a valuable part of your team by recognising their contribution and sharing your vision for the future of the business.

Set up situations to encourage sharing. If your business is reasonably small, informal sharing may take place over drinks on a Friday night. As your business grows, you may need to have more formal structures, such as weekly meetings or individual mentoring sessions.

### Delegate successfully

Successful delegation is a combination of trust and ruthlessness. Give a person a job and leave them to get on with it. Guide them if they ask for help, but don't interfere. You want to train your staff to perform their job well, not train them to think as you do. Nor should you expect them to take the same attitude towards your business as you—after all, for them it is a 'job'. Hopefully a job they like, but still a job.

When your staff members have finished a task, evaluate the results. If they have done well, praise them. If they could have done better, point out the errors and encourage them to do better next time. If their work is unacceptable, don't burden yourself by putting up with them for years and years and praying for them to leave—get rid of them (without falling foul of the employment laws).

At the same time as giving your staff responsibility, you must also mentor them—listening to them and sharing your own experiences. This is an intensive time investment when you have other pressing work to do, but helping your staff improve their skills is an investment for your business.

## Outsource some tasks

Rather than employ staff, you may decide to outsource some of your business tasks. Many small businesses outsource their telemarketing, design work, printing and accounting. Sometimes, as businesses grow bigger, they bring some of these tasks back in-house.

One of the big advantages of outsourcing is flexibility. You may contract services on an 'as needs' basis so you pay for the hours or service you require rather than paying a salary. You can also change suppliers more easily if you need to.

## Record your staff policies

Many small businesses do not record their staff policies because they make an assumption their staff will understand them. This may be the case when your business is small and intimate, but as your business grows you may no longer have the same amount of contact with all your staff.

For example, the partners in an accounting firm believed they had a family-friendly workplace with loyal staff—and for several years they did. But then the firm expanded rapidly over a two-year period and 'loyal' staff started leaving for other jobs. When the human resources manager surveyed the staff, she found they didn't share the partners' perception that the firm was family-friendly. For example, the staff didn't believe they could work from home, leave early for an appointment or take time off for study. The staff retention problem vanished when the firm put its family-friendly policies in writing.

John Pettit makes a point of mentoring his staff in all three stores. He is always available for phone calls and emails, but also makes a formal time each month with every staff member, no matter what their position, for a mentoring session. This investment of time has helped him address staff concerns before they become grudges and also helped his staff develop their skills.

**Blue Gum RESTAURANT**

Tania James and Bill Johnson have good staff relationships as they take a personal interest in all their staff, but at the same time give them a reasonable amount of autonomy. They also provide rigorous training for new staff to ensure they follow all their processes and procedures. They are aware that if they want to go away on holiday more often, they need to delegate some managerial responsibility.

# Finances

Many small business owners set up their business because they love what they do. But all businesses have to pay attention to their finances to be profitable.

When Jane first started her business, she had no interest in finances—as long as she was making enough money, she was happy. She's now learnt that her finances are in better shape if she gives them a higher priority.

## Write a budget

All businesses, whatever their size, need a budget, but it's especially important when you're growing your business. Your budget is a statement of your anticipated sales and expenditure for the year ahead and tells you how much income you need to meet your expenses and make a profit.

You may be tempted to hand over this task to your accountant, but unless your accountant is an integral part of your business, they are not close enough to your goals to draw up your budget. If you delegate the job to a staff member, you must 'own' the final budget so you understand your business's financial situation.

Many small businesses use their previous year's budget as a starting point and adjust the figures to allow for inflation and anticipated changes. This is called 'incremental budgeting'. For a special project, you might decide to start from scratch with what is known as a zero-based approach.

When you're writing your budget, do some 'what if' scenarios. What if you lose a major client? What if you suddenly sold more products than anticipated? Imagine the best and the worst that could happen to your business's finances, then look at how you would cope. Also, think about any risks your business faces and whether you need any additional insurance.

## Develop a cash-flow forecast

All businesses need to manage their cash flow so they have enough money to pay the bills when they come in. If you're not in control of your cash flow, minor problems can escalate and you may find yourself in financial difficulty. Even profitable businesses have gone under because of cash-flow problems.

Cash-flow forecasting is an extension of your budget, but income and expenditure are allocated against a time frame and you don't follow accrual accounting principles. In other words, you record cash when it comes in and goes out, not when you send the invoice or order the supplies.

Most small businesses will find a monthly cash-flow forecast adequate, but if your business has a large number of transactions, you may prefer a weekly or fortnightly forecast. At the end of the period, record your actual figures against the forecast to see how your finances are tracking. Spotting potential cash-flow problems in advance can help you act quickly to avert financial difficulties.

When creating a cash-flow forecast for the first time, look at previous budgets and bank statements to see if there is a clear pattern of income and expenditure. Then consult your current budget to see if, and when, you anticipate making major expenditures.

## Pricing

A big mistake many small business owners make is undercharging for their products and services. Many people seem to think because they don't have large overheads their products and services should be cheaper than those of large organisations. What they forget to take into consideration is that often people are prepared to pay more for your experience and a quicker, more personalised service.

There's also a perception in the marketplace that if you charge a lot your products and services must be high quality. This is particularly true if your products and services are unique. Think about your own attitude towards prices. If you get three quotes for a job, you may go with the middle one rather than the cheapest because you doubt the quality of products and services that are too cheap. Many people I know who've raised their fees find they attract more work as a result. Some clients or customers may beat your price down—but they may also have done that to your previous price.

To determine a fair price for your products and services, look at what your competitors are charging, think about what *you*

John Pettit has always done an annual budget, but had never done a cash-flow forecast until a year ago, when he had cash-flow problems for the first time as a large client was very slow to pay their bill. With the help of his accountant, he has now developed a cash-flow forecast and, as a result, feels much more in control of his finances.

As Bill Johnson is an accountant by profession, budgeting and bookkeeping have not been a problem for the restaurant. However, as the business is growing, he has decided to employ a bookkeeper on a part-time basis so he can take a more active management role.

Managing money is not Jane Amos's strong point, but she knows if she wants to grow her business she needs to pay attention to her finances and manage her money wisely. So she asked her business coach and bookkeeper for advice and, after much procrastination, drew up a budget and a cash-flow forecast.

think your products or services are worth, and discuss your prices with colleagues, prospective buyers and your coach or advisory group.

## Develop new products and services

You may grow your business and increase your profitability by developing new products or services.

### Work with other markets

If you have developed a product or service in one market, you could adapt your offering to suit another market without too much effort. It's easiest to move into a new area where you know some people, so think about who you know, ask them what they need, and then tailor your existing product or service to meet their needs. For example, if you already provide services to accountants, you could offer services to bookkeepers as well.

Don't rule out working with groups who may not normally be able to afford your services, such as small businesses or the not-for-profit sector. One way of working with such groups is finding a sponsor to subsidise your work. For example, if you were running a training seminar for a non-profit organisation, you could ask a corporate client for the use of their training room in exchange for putting their logo on your promotional material and workbooks.

### Bundle your products or services together

Some businesses bundle together products and services, such as training manuals, CDs, books, audiotapes and online learning packages, into what's called an 'infoproduct'. Overall, people get a discount for each item, but as they would seldom buy each item at the one time, you make a larger profit. People will often buy infoproducts after they've heard you speak and are inspired by your speech.

Have a look on the Internet and you'll find many businesses offering infoproducts as well as plenty of other sites offering to help you develop yours.

### Delite Landscape DESIGN

John Pettit has decided to consolidate his balcony design service before introducing anything new. He plans to increase his profits by selling more products and services rather than raising his prices.

### Blue Gum RESTAURANT

Having developed a successful dial-a-dinner service for working people, Tania James and Bill Johnson are thinking about expanding this service to include 'cook a special meal'. Special meals could include Valentine's Day, Christmas, anniversaries and birthdays. This service could be discreet, so the customers' guests needn't know their hosts didn't prepare the meal themselves.

###  Jane Amos NATURAL THERAPIST

Jane Amos plans to make a CD of techniques people can use to relax and heal their own bodies. If the CD sells well, she hopes to write a book.

## Business systems

Michael Gerber, author of *The E-Myth Revisited* (1995), made famous the idea of working *on*, not *in*, your business. Even if you are the only one delivering your service, you need to create integrated systems to make your business more efficient and provide a consistent client experience.

Many small businesses have outdated or inefficient processes that take up too much time. If that's the case in your business, do a stocktake of your current processes and technologies to identify gaps and areas of inefficiency. If you're providing a product or a service that others can deliver without your presence, your business should be able to run efficiently while you're holidaying in Hawaii.

If you need to improve your technology, consult experts and shop around for the best value for money. You must be able to totally rely on your technology not to let you down and have all your computer systems thoroughly backed up. As my IT supplier says: 'It's not a question of *if* you'll have a hard disk failure, it's a question of *when*.' Ideally, you should have your back-up in a separate location from your office.

At the same time as making your business systems more efficient, document them so new staff can refer to them and you can review them regularly. Documenting your systems as you go will also save you from spending hours writing up your systems retrospectively when you sell your business.

When you write your systems, keep them simple. Use either an MS Word document or Excel spreadsheet, or buy specific software. Do the business process itself as you record it, rather than writing notes from memory, and include all relevant forms or screenshots in your document.

Recently, John Pettit's staff started to complain that his computer system was too slow and he realised his computers were four years old and it was time to upgrade them. Upgrading his computers wasn't in his budget but, as sales had been higher than anticipated, John decided to upgrade his computers immediately rather than wait until the next financial year.

One of the reasons Tania James has enrolled in an online restaurant management course is because she wants to improve the restaurant's business systems so she and Bill can take more holidays.

### Jane Amos
**NATURAL THERAPIST**

Jane Amos initially resisted the idea of developing processes and systems for her work, but her coach encouraged her to record her processes for any action in her business she performed more than once. Jane was surprised to find that developing a systematic approach, even to small things such as the way she stored her massage oils, helped her provide her clients with a more professional service. For example, she is no longer rummaging around trying to find things when her clients arrive.

## Celebrate

Inevitably, you will become distracted at times from your big-picture goals by day-to-day issues and minor hassles. So stand back from your business from time to time and acknowledge your achievements. Although plans seldom turn out exactly how you envisage, you'll often be pleasantly surprised to realise how well you are progressing towards your goals.

And don't forget to celebrate your successes!

# References

## Chapter 1    Planning

Brennan, J. H., *How to Get Where You Want To Go*, Thorsons Publishers, UK, revised edition, 1991.

McGrath, John, *You Inc*, HarperCollins Publishers, Sydney, Australia, 2003.

Ziglar, Zig, *Zig Ziglar's Secrets of Closing the Sale*, Berkley Publishing Group, New York, 1984.

## Chapter 2    What do you do?

Middleton, Robert, *InfoGuru Marketing Manual*, www.actionplan.com

Misner, Ivan R. and Morgan, Don, *Masters of Networking: Building relationships for your pocketbook and soul*, Bard Press, Marietta, GA, 2000.

www.aboutpeople.com

www.summitconsulting.com

## Chapter 3   Word of mouth and referrals

Collins, Jim, *Good to Great: Why some companies make the leap... and others don't*, HarperCollins Publishers, New York, 2001.
Gladwell, Malcolm, *The Tipping Point: How little things can make a big difference*, Abacus, London, UK, 2000.
Marsden, Paul, Dr, *The Tipping Point: From dream to reality*, www.brandgenetics.com/archive [2004].
New Zealand Trade and Enterprise, Business Survey Report, Sydney, 2002.
Rogers, Everett M., *Diffusion of Innovations*, 5th edition, Free Press, New York, 2003.
Silverman, George, *The Secrets of Word-of-Mouth Marketing*, AMACOM, New York, 2001.
http://futureswatch.org/TELS_Course/Module_3/Diffusion_of_Innovation4.htm
www.doubleclick.com
www.thedrg.com

## Chapter 4   Networking

Misner, Ivan R. and Morgan, Don, *Masters of Networking: Building relationships for your pocketbook and soul*, Bard Press, Marietta, GA, 2000.
Roane, Susan, *How to Work a Room: A guide to successfully managing the mingling*, Shapolsky Publishers, New York, 1988.
www.networkingtowin.com.au
www.susanroane.com

## Chapter 5   Telemarketing

Hopkins, Tom, *Selling for Dummies*, Wiley Publishing, Inc., New York, 2nd edition, 2001.

Stapleton, James J., *Developing a CPA Practice*, John Wiley & Sons, New York, 1997.
Schiffman, Stephan, *Telesales*, Adams Media Corporation, Avon, MA, 2003.
www.dnb.com
www.kompass.com

## Chapter 6   Public speaking

McCathy, Patsy and Hatcher, Caroline, *Speaking Persuasively: How to make the most of your presentations*, Allen & Unwin, Sydney, Australia, 1996.
Rozakis, Laurie, *The Complete Idiot's Guide to Public Speaking*, Alpha Books, Indianapolis, IN, 1999.
www.fripp.com
www.networkingtowin.com.au
www.nsaspeakers.org
www.pr.mq.edu/au/macnews/may01/croucher.htm
www.summitconsulting.com
www.susanroane.com
www.workinghumor.com/quotes/seinlanguage.shtml

## Chapter 7   Running seminars

Jolles, Robert L., *How to Run Seminars and Workshops*, John Wiley & Sons, New York, 2001.
Maister, David H., *Managing the Professional Services Firm*, Free Press Paperbacks, New York, 1997.
www.anniejenningspr.com
www.paulkarasik.com

## Chapter 8  More ways to talk up your business

Griffiths, Andrew, *101 Ways to Market Your Business*, Allen & Unwin, Sydney, Australia, 2000.
www.ceir.org
www.sharronsenter.com
www.sponsorship.com
www.thetradeshowcoach.com

## Chapter 9  Grow your business from within

Benjamin, Ian, *Consulting, Contracting and Freelancing*, Allen & Unwin, Sydney, Australia, 2003.
Gerber, Michael, *The E-Myth Revisited*, HarperBusiness, New York, 1995.
Misner, Ivan R., and Morgan, Don, *Masters of Success: Proven techniques for achieving success in business and life*, Entrepreneur Press, Canada, 2004.
Peters, Tom, *The Brand You: Fifty ways to transform yourself from an 'employee' into a brand that shouts distinction, commitment and passion*, Alfred A. Knopf, New York, 1999.
Peters, Tom and Waterman, Robert H., *In Search of Excellence: Lessons from America's best-run companies*, Harper & Row, New York, 1982.
Thorpe, Peter, *Success Secrets for Your Small Business*, The Advertising Department, Sydney, Australia, 2004.
Westpac, *Guide for Community Treasurers*, Australia, 2004.
Zhivago, Kristin, *Rivers of Revenue*, Smokin' Donut Books, Jamestown, RI, 2004.
www.entrepreneur.com
www.gemconsortium.org
www.homebizbuzz.co.nz

# Further reading

Findlay Schenck, Barbara, *Small Business Marketing for Dummies*, Hungry Minds, New York, 2001.
Lundin, Stephen C., Paul, Harry and Christensen, John, *Fish!* Hodder & Stoughton, London, UK, 2001.
Rix, Peter, *Marketing: A practical approach*, 5th edition, McGraw-Hill, Sydney, Australia, 2004.

# E-newsletters

www.actionplan.com
www.bly.com
www.briantracey.com
www.clickz.com
www.debbieweil.com
www.emarketer.com
www.marketingprofs.com
www.marketingsherpa.com

# Index

accelerate buying process *see* buying process, accelerate
action plan 13–14
advisory board 166–7
affiliate program 52
after-service 43–5
Amos, Jane, natural therapist xi–xii
  action plan 14
  after-service 45
  belief in services 10
  CD 175
  coach, personal 167
  column, newspaper 158
  community involvement 152
  context 37

elevator statements 18, 20–2, 24, 26
endorsed letter 51
finances 170, 173
goals 12
keep in touch 41
networking 56, 59, 65, 70, 72, 76
public speaking 107, 108–9, 111–13, 119, 125–6
referrals 49 *see also* word of mouth *and* endorsed letter
resistances 7
seminars 132, 143, 147, 149
special customers 43
systems, business 177

telemarketing 84, 86, 92–6, 100, 102–3
training 164
word of mouth 37–8 *see also* referrals *and* endorsed letter

Blue Gum Restaurant xi
  advisory board 167
  affiliate program 52
  after-service 45
  belief, in business 8–10
  benefits and solutions 20–4
  bookkeeping 173
  community involvement 151
  connectors 35, 69
  elevator statements 20–5
  goals 6, 12
  networking 56, 58, 75
  public speaking 106, 110, 112, 115, 124–5
  radio 157
  referrals 49
  review 3–4
  seminars 131, 146, 149
  special customers 43
  special meals 175
  sponsorship 154
  staff training 159, 164, 170
  systems 40, 177

telemarketing 83, 85, 91–2, 94–5
budget 171–4
business cards 62–3
business coaching *see* coaching
business review *see* review business
business systems *see* systems, business
buying process, accelerate 39–40

call tracking 97–103
capitalise on *see* follow up
cash-flow forecast 171–3
Centre for Exhibition Industry Research (CEIR) 155
charge for, seminars 129–32
closing speeches 116
coaching, 164–7
Collins, Jim 37
columns, newspapers and magazines 157–8
commission for referrals 50
community 55–6, 145–7, 150–2
conferences 156–7
connectors 34–7, 68–9
contact sheet, telemarketing 88

context, power of 36–7
continual improvement 163–5
customer service 159
Customer Value Proposition (CVP) 2
customers, special 42–3

database 63–4, 71, 84–7, 107, 135, 148
delegate 168–9
Delite Landscape Design x–xi
  after-service 44
  answering phone 28
  business coach 164, 167
  cash-flow forecast 173
  community involvement 151
  continual improvement, *see* business coach
  elevator statements 19, 21–3, 26 *see also* introductions
  goals 11
  introductions 28–9 *see also* elevator statements
  name tags 66
  networking 56, 58, 71, 75
  profits, increase 175
  public speaking 106, 108, 110, 112, 117–18, 124, 126
  radio 158

referrals 48
review 5
s-curve 38
seminars 130, 141, 146, 148
special customers 43
sponsorship 154
staff 42, 159, 170
sticky product 36
systems, business 177
telemarketing 83–5, 91–5
trade shows 156
Dieringer Research Group 39
DoubleClick 39

early adopters 33
early majority 33
elevator pitch *see* elevator statements
elevator statements 15–30, 62 *see also* introductions
endorsed letter 51
e-newsletters 73, 123, 137–8
evaluation forms 142–4
experience, learn from 165
eye contact, speeches 121–2

failure
  fear of 78–9
  reasons for 59–61, 78–81
filing system *see* database
finances 170–4
flywheel 37–8

# Index

follow up 25–7, 70–3, 122–5
    *see also* after-service

gatekeepers 90
Gerber, Michael 176
gifts 51–2
Gladwell, Malcolm 32–6
goals 10–13
good listener *see* listener
groups, networking 57–9

IEG, Inc. 152
improvement, continual *see* continual improvement
infoproduct 174–5
innovators 33
introductions
    group 27–8
    speaker 29–30
    types of 19–24
invitations 144–5

joint ventures 50

Kennedy, John 119

labels 19–20 *see also* elevator statements
laggards 33–4
late majority 33
Lions 107
list, the 84–6

listener, good 68
live seminars *see* seminars
loyalty program 42–3

Maister, David H. 127, 133–4
MarketingSherpa 137–8
mavens 34
measurement 74–5, 97–103, 125–6, 148–9
media releases *see* press releases
mentor *see* coaching
messages, leaving 97
Misner and Morgan 27
monitor *see* measurement
movement, speeches 121–2

name tags 66
National Speakers Association 110
networking 53–76
New Zealand Trade & Enterprise 31
    at the event 64–70
    online 73–4
niche market 4

online research *see* research
openings, speeches 115–16
outsource 169

partner 160 *see also* joint ventures
patience 162
persistence *see* patience
phone, answering 28 *see also* telemarketing
pictures, visual 24
planning 1–14
  introduction 62
  networking 54–6, 61–3
  public speaking 105–7
  seminars 138–9
  speech 113–15
  telemarketing 81–2
policies, record 169
politically correct 119–20
Post-it-Notes 36–7
PowerPoint 140
practise
  answering phone 28
  speech 120
  telephone script 91, 97
preparation *see* planning
press releases 145
pricing 172–4
problems
  relate answer to 21–2
  speech structure 114
Probus groups 38, 107–8, 118
professional services, seminars for 133–4
profile, write 29–30, 112–13
proposal, speaking 109
public speaking 104–26

questions, open-ended 93–4

radio 145, 157–8
referrals 46–52
referrer 47, 68–9 *see also* referrals
repetition 119
research 39–40, 82–3, 153
resistances 6–7
review business 3–6
Rogers, Everett M. 33–4
Rotary 107

salespeople 34 *see also* staff
Salespeople With A Purpose *see* SWAP
Schiffman, Stephan 80
Script, telemarketing 90–1
s-curve 32–9
Seinfeld, Jerry 105
seminars 127–149
  types of 132–6
Sesame Street 35
Silver, Dr Spence 36
small talk 67
speaking topics 109–12
special customers *see* customers, special
special offer 123–4

speech writing tips *see* writing tips, speeches
speeches, structure 114–15
sponsorship 152–4
staff 41–2, 159, 168–70
Stapleton, James 79, 81, 98
statistics 118–19
sticky product 35
stories 26–7, 117–18, 141
structure, speeches 114–15
   *see also* telemarketing, conversation
subcontract 50
supporters, acknowledge 46
surveys *see* research
SWAP 57, 107
SWOT 2
systems, business 176–7
   *see also* telemarketing

telemarketing 77–103
  conversation 91–6
teleseminars 135–8

television *see* TV
thank you, cards, letters and notes 46, 71–2
time management 87, 89
tipping point 32–5
Toastmasters 113
trade shows 154–6
training staff *see* staff
Trivial Pursuit 34–5
TV 157–9

Unique Selling Proposition (USP) 2, 17

voice 121–2

webinars 134–7
word of mouth 31–46
writing tips, speeches 116–20

'yes' ladder 95–6

Ziglar, Zig 9

## ALSO FROM ALLEN & UNWIN

*PROMOTE YOUR BUSINESS*
*How to write effective marketing material*
*for your small business*
**Mary Morel**

Need to promote your business? Of course you do.

But you don't need to hire an expensive copywriter or public relations agency. With the help of this book, you can write your own promotional material that is effective, looks great and doesn't cost a fortune.

Whether you're just starting out, or you've been in business for years, *Promote Your Business* is a handy tool to help you write your own:

- advertisements
- brochures
- press releases
- direct mail
- e-newsletters
- websites.

This is a must read for anyone in small business who wants to write marketing material that makes their products or services stand out. You'll save time and money and, best of all, help your customers know more about your business.

ISBN 1 86508 931 1